What People Are S

"Michael McKeldon Woody captures the essence of the forces that have caused the net annual loss of jobs to offshore to drop from about 150,000 ten years ago to zero today. If companies follow Michael's principles and understand the total cost of offshoring, they will reshore another million jobs now."

Harry Moser
Founder, The Reshoring Initiative

"*American Dragon* and the principles of *fewer*, *faster*, and *finer* are a road map for helping US manufacturers beat the imports."

Margarita Mendoza
Founder, Made in America Movement

"As the founder of a small but growing US brand, I've been greatly encouraged by Michael McKeldon Woody's insights."

Isabelle Benoit
Founder and President, Bullet Blues Custom Apparel

"*American Dragon's* principles of *fewer*, *faster*, and *finer* dovetail with the lean principles I espouse in my business and provide a game plan that small to midsize manufacturers can use to compete more effectively with overseas companies."

Karl Wadensten
President, Vibco Industries

"In order for the United States to return to and remain a prosperous nation, we need to revitalize our manufacturing base. Michael Woody's *American Dragon* is a great forum for manufacturing execs to share our ideas toward that common goal."

Cathy Williams-Owen
President, Drimark Products

"How fortunate we are to have someone of Michael McKeldon Woody's caliber to write a clear exposition of the industry that was, the industry that is, and the industry that will be."

Mark Gilman
Chairman of the Board, Gill Studios
Former Chairman of the Board,
Promotional Products Association International

AMERICAN DRAGON

Winning the Global Manufacturing War Using the Universal Principles of *Fewer, Faster,* and *Finer*

Michael McKeldon Woody

Copyright © 2016 Michael McKeldon Woody.
Associated logos are trademarks and/or registered
trademarks of Michael McKeldon Woody.

All rights reserved. No part of this book may be reproduced, stored, or transmitted by any means—whether auditory, graphic, mechanical, or electronic—without written permission of both publisher and author, except in the case of brief excerpts used in critical articles and reviews. Unauthorized reproduction of any part of this work is illegal and is punishable by law.

ISBN: 978-1-4834-4576-2 (sc)
ISBN: 978-1-4834-4577-9 (hc)
ISBN: 978-1-4834-4575-5 (e)

Library of Congress Control Number: 2016901238

Because of the dynamic nature of the Internet, any web addresses or links contained in this book may have changed since publication and may no longer be valid. The views expressed in this work are solely those of the author and do not necessarily reflect the views of the publisher, and the publisher hereby disclaims any responsibility for them.

Lulu Publishing Services rev. date: 03/01/2016

*For my wife, Joanne,
who kept this dream alive*

There is a tide in the affairs of men,
Which, taken at the flood, leads on to fortune;
Omitted, all the voyage of their life
Is bound in shallows and in miseries.
On such a full sea are we now afloat,
And we must take the current when it serves,
Or lose our ventures.

—William Shakespeare
Julius Caesar, Act 4, Scene 3

CONTENTS

Acknowledgments xi
Introduction xiii

Chapter 1 *Fewer, Faster,* and *Finer*—Exploit Weakness 1
Chapter 2 The Tale of Two Companies—Living in the Best
           and Worst of Times 19
Chapter 3 The Enemy Within—Extinguish the Fire 38
Chapter 4 The Making of Less—Producing *Fewer* 55
Chapter 5 The Speed Merchants—Moving *Faster* 73
Chapter 6 The Best in Class—Manufacturing *Finer* 90
Chapter 7 The Power of We—Building Great Teams 107
Chapter 8 A Small Price to Pay—The Role of the Consumer
           and B2B Buyer 124
Chapter 9 The Power to Persevere—Government Must Lead,
           Follow or Get Out of the Way 136

Conclusion: The Recession-Proof Business 157
Index 163
Endnotes 167

ACKNOWLEDGMENTS

Some of the company names in this book have been changed because the owners or managers of those companies wished to remain anonymous. Why? Because they either currently sell into China or hope to eventually sell into China, and they fear being blackballed. Even one of the major publishers who expressed interest in the manuscript asked if I could "tone down the China rhetoric" because they sell a lot of books in China. These incidents only confirmed the importance of *American Dragon*'s message, so I thank the reluctant for the extra motivation.

As a combination of personal history and how-to book, *American Dragon* is a bit of an anomaly. When I started down this path, I wasn't sure if balancing these two approaches in a business book would even make sense, much less be readable. A number of people were kind enough to look over my drafts, some conversant in manufacturing and/or the promotional products industry and some not. All provided reassurance that I was on the right track. Their encouragement kept me writing and revising.

Patricia Slonina Vieira read my first draft and provided support very early in the process. Kent Gladding, an investment professional, read one of my final drafts and reassured me that a layperson could understand both my descriptions of how and why offshoring occurred and the somewhat Byzantine nature of the promotional products distribution network. Steve Yukel went over my final draft with a fine-tooth comb, a critically important task given that I had lived with some sections of the text for over three years. Mark Gilman, Wayne Roberts, and Gene Geiger, promotional products industry veterans, confirmed my recollection of how and why promotional products were offshored. Rick Brenner's extensive background knowledge on the Consumer Products Safety Improvement

Act was essential to my explanation of the importance of the *finer* principle. I imposed on a new friend, Fr. Bill Miscamble, to look at a near-final draft, and he served as my third-base coach, waving me home.

Thank you, Michele Bell at the Advertising Specialty Institute, for access to old archives on the promotional products industry. A nod to Sarah Butler for helping me ramp up the *American Dragon* social media machine. To Pat and Michael Snell—we didn't make it happen this time, but you made me a better writer and our paths will cross again. To my friend Brandon Mackay, for his support and for the story that remains untold.

There were several books I encountered along the way that served as both inspiration and motivation. Chief among them are:

Re-Made in the USA—Todd Lipscomb's account of his journey that led to the creation of www.madeinusaforever.com.

Strategic Capitalism—Richard D'Aveni's warning of the strategic threat that China's form of capitalism represents, and how the United States should respond.

The Long Tail—Chris Anderson's seminal book on the effects of technology on product demand and distribution was essential to my explanation of the *fewer* principle.

Factory Man—Beth Macy's history of the Bassett Furniture empire shows that one person can make a difference.

Producing Prosperity—Gary Pisano and Willy Shih make the case that without manufacturing, we lose our capacity to innovate; and if we cease to innovate, what remains?

Finally, a tip of the hat to Harry Moser's Reshoring Initiative, the Made in America Movement, USA Love List, Makers Row, the Job Shop Company, and so many other organizations that continue to relentlessly trumpet the importance of US manufacturing.

INTRODUCTION

The American Industrial Revolution

It is a little-known fact that the American industrial revolution was started by a copycat—a brilliant one, but a copycat nonetheless. To evade British law, he wore a farmer's costume and clandestinely boarded a boat headed to the newly formed United States of America.

It was the late eighteenth century, and the industrial revolution in England was running full throttle. The textile industry at that time was driven by the water-powered spinning machines used to convert cotton into yarn, which eventually became fabric. But the lion's share of the raw cotton used in British textile mills happened to be imported from US cotton farmers. The British government, in order to prevent US companies from hijacking the spinning machine technology and setting up similar mills, passed laws forbidding their textile workers from traveling to America.

A young Samuel Slater, after working as an apprentice in a textile mill for seven years, envisioned a life in the New World. So he donned his farmer's disguise and snuck aboard a ship to the United States, bringing with him the technology that would spark the American industrial revolution. With a booming population, plenty of land for expansion, and a wealth of natural resources, the United States eventually became the manufacturer to the world, churning out the commodity products that everyone wanted. By the end of World War II, our standard of living was the world's highest.

But then the war-ravaged economies of Europe and Asia recovered. Germany and Japan, aided by the Marshall Plan, ramped up their own manufacturing capabilities. High-quality German and low-priced Japanese products began to enter the United States. Economists were teaching that globalization is good. They calculated that importing lower-priced goods from overseas would drive our living standards ever higher. The number of trade deals multiplied, and US tariffs were lowered.

In 1989, two hundred years after Slater's journey, manufacturers from China were visiting US trade shows and factories, researching the hottest products and how they were made, then taking the manufacturing know-how home and using reverse engineering to make those products at one third the price. How? By paying extremely low wages to workers toiling in often dangerous working conditions, and paying little heed to environmental pollution. Faced with competition from these lower-wage countries, US manufacturers responded by making ever cheaper products, often sacrificing quality in the process.

Meanwhile, US-based multinationals, brands, and big-box retailers began offshoring production of goods to the lowest-cost country. Bangladesh outbid China for the "privilege" of making the world's T-shirts in sweatshop conditions that were outlawed in the United States a century ago. India, Vietnam, Pakistan, and others entered the manufacturing fray. The United States passed NAFTA, and then, at the turn of the new millennium, China, with US support, entered the World Trade Organization (WTO). Over the next decade, six million US manufacturing jobs were lost. And I was part of the problem.

"These Chinese pens are not a threat," I remember telling my sales rep, Ron, at a 1992 trade show in Dallas. Shaking his head, Ron quickly shepherded me over to the pens that one of our competitors was importing from China. He picked up a pen to show me how poorly made this nonbranded pen was, offered at half the price of our finely crafted, lifetime-guaranteed Quill pens. The Chinese import was light as a feather—not a good thing for a "quality" metal pen—with a matte finish thin enough to rub off. The mechanism for projecting the pen's point was creaky, and instead of writing smoothly, it felt scratchy.

At that time, I was vice president of international sales and marketing at the Quill Company, a US writing instrument manufacturer based in Providence, Rhode Island. Quill, a textbook example of a small family-owned company, produced a quality product that served a niche in the expanding promotional products market and grew steadily throughout the 1980s. By the early 1990s, sales were still trending up, but our growth had leveled off. At the time I attributed this largely to the 1990s' recession, but Ron disagreed.

He took me down another aisle to a different competitor selling a Chinese pen identical to the one I had just seen. Now I understood: the China manufacturer was selling the same pen to multiple US importers using long production runs. Those long runs and mediocre quality standards allowed them to sell at much lower prices than Quill. Ron warned me that these pens were eating into our market share. Still, I was certain that no buyer would opt for such a poorly made product from China over a US-made product with a lifetime guarantee—even at half the price. I was dead wrong.

By the time I started my own consulting business ten years later, the triumph of China imports was so resounding that I had acquiesced in the inevitability of US companies sourcing in China. I actually encouraged it to clients and to audiences at presentations throughout the world.

Then in 2006 I stumbled onto a small company in the textile business, Trans-Tex LLC. This company provided me with an opportunity for a rematch with my old nemesis, China, with an entirely different result. During the worst economic environment since the Great Depression, this small manufacturer in an old-school industry had battled and beaten the imports by implementing the three simple principles of *fewer, faster,* and *finer*.

1. *Fewer* means shorter, more-customized production runs.
2. *Faster* means quicker production lead times.
3. *Finer* means higher-quality, safer products.

These principles are effective because they attack the increasingly glaring weaknesses in the China manufacturing business model: steadily rising prices, geographic distance, poor grasp of US product safety guidelines, the threat of intellectual property theft, and an emphasis on long production runs of commodity products.

As I began reading about other companies exploiting these weaknesses to successfully compete with imports, I realized that they, too, were relying heavily on the principles of *fewer, faster,* and *finer*. It became apparent that other struggling US manufacturers, battered by the flood of low-cost imports and believing that all is lost, would benefit from these stories. So I wrote this book to coach and encourage us to keep fighting the good fight.

How important is this battle? As we struggle to rise from the ashes of the worst economic downturn since the Great Depression, an unemployment rate that peaked at 10.8 percent has now dropped below 6 percent. Think we're out of the woods? Not a chance. Wage levels remain stagnant, with increases driven more by state governments raising minimum pay than by a strong job market and increasing productivity. The Wall Street Journal noted that wage growth for hourly wage earners remains "tepid," and the share of Americans participating in the labor force (62.6 percent) matches the lowest reading since 1977.[1] Many prospective workers have simply given up their job search.

There is a chorus of voices that say that the state of manufacturing in the United States is fine and that we are simply more productive and need fewer workers to produce the same results. Yes, our manufacturing sector is more productive. But this is little solace to those whose jobs have been lost not to automation, but to offshoring. According to some estimates, over two million US manufacturing jobs have been exported to China alone since the turn of the century. And although we are more productive, our position as the world's leader in manufacturing output is slipping. Since 1990, China has passed France, Italy, the United Kingdom, Germany, and Japan, and is bearing down on us. Some say that China has already passed the United States in manufacturing output.[2]

Keep in mind that the loss of our manufacturing base also leaves us vulnerable to strategic threats. Why? Because manufacturing drives innovation and innovation drives manufacturing. If we lose the capacity to manufacture, even in basic industries, we will lose the capacity to innovate. As the MIT Task Force on Innovation and Production succinctly puts it, "the loss of companies that make things will end up in the loss of research that can invent them."[3] And that loss means the loss of millions more jobs and a gradual decay in our quality of life and ability as a country to counter strategic threats. Recreating those manufacturing capabilities, once lost, is difficult, if not impossible.

In their book *Producing Prosperity*, Gary Pisano and Willy Shih describe industrial commons as "webs of technological knowhow, operational capabilities, and specialized skills that are embedded in the workforce, competitors, suppliers, customers, cooperative R&D ventures, and universities and often support multiple industrial sectors."[4] They go on to explain that when an industrial commons erodes, the foundation for future innovation is damaged because it is more difficult to design new products or improve existing products when the manufacturing environment is a continent away from research and development. Reshoring an industry is not as simple as opening up a factory to build a particular product.

The manufacturing of a product does not occur at one building or even in one company. Typically, a chain of vendors exists that supports a manufacturer in construction of the final product. Manufacturing is a sequential process involving a number of different types of companies. When we lose all or most of the pieces of that chain to other countries, reshoring the manufacturing of that product is almost impossible unless we reshore all or most of the components in that chain.

Apparel is a good example. The manufacturing channel for apparel includes brands, designers, contractors, yarn producers, fabric manufacturers, cut and sew operations, and packaging companies. To cost-effectively bring apparel manufacturing back to the United States requires that *all* of these elements be reshored in geographic clusters that can efficiently compete with overseas sources.

Isabelle Benoit is the owner and founder of Bullet Blues Custom Apparel, a boutique apparel company that manufactures all of its clothing from US-made fabrics and accessories. She grew up not in the cornfields of the Midwest or the streets of Los Angeles, but in Southwestern France. When she came to the United States and decided to start Bullet Blues, she was determined that her line would be totally made in the United States of America. Why? Because as she was coming of age across the Atlantic, Isabelle had always admired the quality of US-made product. More importantly, her business model and company name are a tribute to the US soldiers who rest in the graves at Normandy.

Her main challenge as a start-up was finding quality fabric and accessories (buttons, zippers, etc.) manufactured in the United States. Fabric manufacturing had emigrated overseas, taking with it the cut and sew operations and accessories manufacturers, as well as the contractors who pulled the entire package together. Although she overcame this obstacle over time, eventually designing a product line composed exclusively of US-manufactured fabrics and accessories, it took her months to locate vendors. The apparel manufacturing supply chain that existed in the United States forty years earlier had virtually disappeared, and Isabelle, a small business owner with a dream, was forced to cobble one together.

To use a sports metaphor, it is time for us as a nation to protect our home court. The United States remains the world's largest economy, and marketplaces are evolving in ways that favor manufacturing companies in close proximity to their customers that can deliver smaller quantities quickly and that understand the importance of providing safe, reliable products. If you are a small to midsize US manufacturer and you implement the principles of *fewer, faster,* and *finer,* you will position your company to win back customers who made the decision years ago that they would buy from overseas countries based strictly on the fact that they offered the lowest price per piece.

This book was not written to bash our overseas competitors. Its aim is not to denigrate factories in other countries or the people who work in those factories. This book is about people like Isabelle Benoit who follow their dream of starting a business with the goal of labeling their product "Made in the U.S.A." They are my team. I wrote this book in hopes of coaching them and their companies about how to tackle a tough competitor and beat them at their own game. That's not xenophobia. It's showing my support and encouragement for the home team, Team U.S.A.

As an entrepreneur or business owner, if overseas manufacturers have taken your US customers—even in a basic manufacturing industry—this story is proof that you can take those customers back. The principles of *fewer, faster,* and *finer* are driving success at Trans-Tex and many other companies, and they will help you win, too.

CHAPTER 1

Fewer, Faster, and *Finer*— Exploit Weakness

Without strategy you cannot control your opponent.[5]
The Art of War

Imagine if you could replace a garden hose connector by simply pushing the rubber hose into the new connector and having it lock into place with a leak-proof seal. Then imagine that you could fix a leaky connection in your basement plumbing in exactly the same way, with no tools—and that you could remove it with a twist of the wrist. Quick Fitting Inc., a Rhode Island manufacturer, created this new "push to connect" fitting system, which is a quick, convenient way to connect pipes and accessories for plumbing and heating systems. Back in 2010, the company had orders in hand for this newly patented product from a major home goods chain. David Crompton, Quick Fitting's CEO, was concerned that if they manufactured the part in their China factory, quality would suffer, the minimum order size would be too large, and lead times would be too extended due to transoceanic shipping and customs requirements. So he decided to reshore manufacturing to a plant in Warwick, Rhode Island, and hire 200 new employees in a state that, at the time, had the highest unemployment rate in the country.

"We want to have a made-in-the-USA product, and we believe we can make it faster and more efficiently here," said Crompton. He cited higher quality and increased speed in both manufacturing and distribution to his customers as the advantages of manufacturing in Rhode Island rather than China. Crompton was also concerned about the theft of his intellectual property if he manufactured this revolutionary product at a China factory.[6]

Clearly, Quick Fitting's decision to reshore, like that of so many other US companies, was precipitated not only by patriotism. A number of relatively recent macroeconomic developments are transforming distribution networks and supply chains worldwide and weakening the ability of overseas manufacturers to compete with smaller, more nimble domestic manufacturers for customers in the world's largest market, the United States of America. These developments include:

1. The demand of both the consumer and B2B buyer for smaller order sizes and/or more customized product.
2. The need for speed to market.
3. The need for quicker cash cycles in a tough economic environment.
4. The rise of product quality as a brand differentiator.
5. The enactment of stricter product safety regulations in both the United States and the European markets

This combination of factors is exposing a number of vulnerabilities in the traditional overseas manufacturing business model. What were once the greatest strengths of China manufacturers, for example, have now become their biggest weaknesses. In the 1990s the overriding factor for US importers and consumers was the price of the product, and China in particular responded to this low price imperative by constructing a lumbering manufacturing juggernaut that threw millions of low-paid workers at making cheap commodity products by performing mindlessly repetitive tasks in factories that were, by US standards, unsafe.

But the business environment has evolved to favor speed, flexibility, quality, and innovation over price. Companies that can deliver quickly, that can manufacture shorter runs of more customized products, and that produce high-quality, safe products now have the edge. As these attributes become increasingly essential, supply chains will geographically compress, which favors domestic manufacturers. In short, China's manufacturing juggernaut, and those from other low-wage countries that hope to displace

China, will be forced to convert from power players to finesse players—and China will be forced to do it as they face cost increases that are unprecedented in their short history as a manufacturing powerhouse. The resulting upward pressure on the price of goods from China is a dagger to the heart of their traditional value proposition—and that of the many upstarts following their blueprint.

Going Up?
Why the Price of China Goods Will Continue to Rise

The Harwood Company is a major importer of goods from China for resale in the US promotional products market. For decades, importing suppliers in that market have published a catalog each January with pricing established for the full calendar year. However, as the cost of finished goods from China began steadily rising after 2005, Harwood and several other larger importers in that market began printing a midyear catalog to cope with the constant price increases from their China sources. In an industry already burdened with shrinking margins, printing and distributing an additional 100,000 copies of a two-hundred-page, four-color catalog is a sizable expense. However, it was deemed to have less of an impact on the bottom line than keeping prices steady for the full year and absorbing the almost monthly price increases from China.

China's rise as a manufacturing juggernaut was built on the foundation of providing the lowest possible price by using abundant cheap labor to produce long runs of commodity products. The business model is, basically, a lot of people performing the same manual task on the same widget over and over again for very little pay. But over the course of the last decade, China's price advantage has been slowly yet inexorably evaporating. According to an April 2014 report from the Boston Consulting Group, China's pricing advantage over US manufacturers had shrunk to 5 percent.[7] It is common knowledge that US importers of parts and finished goods are dealing with regular and sometimes dramatic increases in the cost of manufactured goods from China. Those price hikes are due to a number of factors, including dramatic increases in labor costs, the strengthening of China's currency against the US dollar, rising oil prices, rising concerns among the Chinese people about air and water pollution caused by manufacturers, and the bursting of the real estate bubble in China.

Hey, Boss, Can I Get a Raise?
Higher Labor Costs

In August 2012, the *Wall Street Journal* reported that labor costs in China had risen 150 percent since 2004.[8] Most analysts expect this trend to continue. During that same year, wages in China's Pearl River Delta, considered the geographic heartland for China manufacturing, rose 10.4 percent.[9] A 2011 Boston Consulting Group study predicted that wage and benefit increases of 15 to 20 percent per year would cut China's cost advantage over wages in lower-cost US states from 55 percent in 2012 to 39 percent in 2015.[10] By the spring of 2014, Harold Sirkin from BCG noted that, "for every dollar required to manufacture in the U.S., it now costs 96¢ to manufacture in China, before considering the cost of transportation to the U.S. and other factors. For many companies, that's hardly worth it when product quality, intellectual property rights, and long-distance supply chain issues are added to the equation."[11]

Much of this increase in China labor costs is driven by the simple law of supply and demand. According to the Asian Development Bank, the working-age population in China increased from 407 million in 1978 to 786 million in 2004. This surge in population created a huge supply of cheap manual labor at precisely the same time that China was ramping up its manufacturing and exporting capabilities. But the one-child policy, instituted in 1979 to stem population growth, had an unforeseen consequence: it has led to a precipitous decline in the number of new laborers entering the workforce. In 1975, there were six children for every elder in China; by 2035, if present trends continue, there will be one child for every two elders. The working-age population is expected to decline by seven million per year through at least 2020.[12]

In November 2013, when it finally recognized the approaching demographic train wreck, the Chinese government loosened the one-child policy, allowing an estimated eleven million couples to apply for approval to have a second child. But the expected baby boom did not materialize. Officials predicted the new policy would lead to two million new births annually, yet in 2014 only 804,000 couples applied to have a second child.[13] By 2015, the fertility rate, which in 1950 had been 6.11 per woman, dropped to 1.55. In response, the government in November 2015 announced a shift to a two-child policy, but many demographers consider it too little, too late. The United Nations is projecting that the number of Chinese over the age of sixty-five will almost double by 2030, from 131 million to 243 million.[14]

The one-child policy also exacerbated a cultural preference for male descendants, so the new, smaller workforce is predominantly male. For every one hundred female births in China, there are now 124 male births, and in some provinces the ratio is even higher.[15] As the number of total available laborers decreases and the ratio of male to female increases, the workforce will become more demanding, increasingly mobile, and more willing to change jobs to chase higher pay.

Foxconn is a massive manufacturing and assembly operation in China that is second only to Walmart in total employees.[16] They are known primarily as a key piece of the supply chain for Apple's iPhone. In 2013 it was reported that 24,000 workers quit each month in their Shenzhen Longhua facility.[17]

The increasingly male-dominated workforce is also becoming more militant. Over two thousand workers at a Foxconn factory caused widespread damage in September 2012 when they rioted and clashed with five thousand police officers dispatched to the scene. Explanations for the riot ranged from a conflict between workers from different provinces to dissatisfaction with pay and working conditions.[18]

In April 2014, more than thirty thousand workers at a Taiwanese-owned shoe factory in the southern province of Guangdong went on strike to protest the company's failure to pay full social security and housing fund contributions. The factory produces athletic footwear for brands such as Adidas, Nike, Reebok, and Timberland.[19] The strike is further evidence of the rising cost of labor in China caused by a shortage of migrant workers and the increasing militancy of China's factory workers. Both factors help to level the playing field for US manufacturers competing with China by putting upward pressure on wages.

At the same time that the labor force is shrinking, the number of jobs in higher-paying manufacturing industries in China is increasing. According to a 2011 report from consulting firm Accenture, average hourly wages for manufacturing workers in both the telecommunications and heavy manufacturing industries are 50 to 60 percent higher than wages in more traditional light manufacturing.[20] One importer told me that the China factory from which he once sourced his line of relatively inexpensive tote bags was forced to shut down for a time after the 2012 Chinese New Year because most of the workers simply did not return after the holiday. He presumed that most of the employees had taken jobs in other, better-paying industries.

As the shrinking workforce in China shifts to higher-paying manufacturing jobs in the automotive and high-tech industries, companies in light manufacturing will be forced to pay higher wages simply to keep workers. These rapidly rising wages are creating an expanding middle class, and as factories increasingly turn to satisfying their demands, less factory capacity and labor will focus on exports. Will China's anemic birthrate of the last twenty years continue to provide an adequate labor force to service both domestic *and* overseas markets? Keep in mind that most businesses will follow the path of least resistance, and it is always easier to service a domestic market than an overseas one. My bet is that China manufacturers will service the domestic market first.

Media attention to dangerous or unfair working conditions at overseas factories has also played a role in increasing labor costs at those factories. Major brands and big-box retailers are now paying closer attention to the working conditions at factories in their supply chain to prevent adverse publicity. Even before the tragic Tazreen factory fire[21] in Bangladesh, Apple had been putting pressure on their largest supplier in China, Foxconn, to improve wages and working conditions at its factories. This is largely due to a series of suicides and labor riots at their factories and the subsequent bad publicity. In October 2014, the US Department of Labor reported that over 168 million children (a number that equals half the population of the United States!) are working in factories around the world, many of them forced to do so, and toiling in deplorable slave labor conditions.[22] Multinational brands and big-box retailers can no longer turn a blind eye to such atrocities, given the glaring light of social media.

It is likely that the emphasis in China's current five-year plan on developing "strategic emerging industries" such as biotechnology, high-end equipment manufacturing, and clean energy vehicles is simply making a virtue out of necessity. In the near future, factory workers available and willing to take lower-paying light assembly jobs in traditional manufacturing industries will be few and far between. The labor shortage in China, and resulting increases in labor costs, will continue to put upward pressure on the price of manufactured goods coming from China for years to come. Only time will tell, but not even a tightly controlled economy like China's can suspend the law of supply and demand indefinitely.

But why wouldn't importers simply shift their procurement to other emerging Pacific Rim manufacturing countries such as Vietnam? What about India or Africa? The problem with this scenario is that most of the countries hoping to land what has traditionally been China business do not currently have the infrastructure (highways, rail lines, ports) that are essential to moving the flood of goods that have been pouring out of China over the last fifteen years.

Money Talks
China Currency Appreciation

US presidential candidates tend to be China hawks during election season and then turn to doves once in office. Bill Clinton dubbed China's leaders "the butchers of Beijing" during the 1992 campaign and later pushed to grant China permanent normal trade relations status *and* negotiated their entry into the World Trade Organization (WTO). Both moves helped to facilitate China's emergence as a manufacturing juggernaut.

This tendency on the part of presidents to soften on China after taking office has led to a balancing act in DC, in which Congress generally acts as the "bad cop" on China while the administration acts as the "good cop." This scenario was playing out in 2006 between Congress and the Bush administration over China's currency peg to the US dollar. Congress wanted Bush to pressure China into floating its currency, releasing its peg to the dollar and letting it rise to its appropriate market level. Some estimated that the yuan was roughly 40 percent undervalued. This meant that the Chinese government was keeping the price of China's exports 40 percent lower than it should be and providing China manufacturers with a huge pricing advantage over their US competitors.[23]

At the time, many of my clients were importing finished goods from China, and I had become resigned to the fact that the drain of manufacturing jobs to China would continue unabated. I even published a magazine article arguing that floating the yuan was a terrible idea that would be disastrous for US companies importing from China because the cost of my clients' purchases would spike dramatically. My recommendation was that Congress and the administration focus on more "important" China issues such as intellectual property rights and North Korean nukes. Ten years later, we've made little progress on either IP or nukes, but China currency has actually strengthened over 25 percent.

US government policy attempts to keep pressure on China to let its currency strengthen but always stops short of calling China a currency manipulator. In February 2013, Treasury Secretary nominee Jack Lew stated during his confirmation hearing that the yuan was undervalued.[24] Then in April 2013, the US Treasury, in a report to Congress on exchange rate policies, echoed Lew's statement by noting that although China had taken measures to make its exchange rate somewhat more flexible, their currency should be allowed to strengthen further to bring it more in line with its fair market value.[25]

In April 2014, Ron Wyden (D-OR), then the newly named chair of the Senate Finance Committee—which oversees US trade policy—noted that the United States should take a tougher stand against currency manipulation by trading partners (e.g., China).[26] Five days later, the Treasury Department, in one of its twice-yearly reports to Congress, announced that China was not a currency manipulator, but that the Peoples Bank of China's policies suggested "continued actions to impede market determination." This type of wordplay has been typical of how Washington's strategy is to pressure China on currency manipulation without pushing too hard.

Although this strategy has led to strengthening of the yuan over time, it's not happening quickly enough for the millions of unemployed and underemployed former factory workers here in the United States. However, as long as US unemployment remains relatively high and/or wages continue to stagnate, Congress is likely to continue its pressure on China to let its currency float to its fair market value, and China is likely to respond over time by allowing the yuan's gradual strengthening to continue. This will maintain constant upward pressure on the price of manufactured goods imported into the United States from China.

Over a Barrel
Oil Price Volatility

Volatile oil prices expose another weakness in the China manufacturing business model. In 2003 a barrel of oil was priced at $28. By July 2008, it was trading at over $140; as of December 2015 it was trading back in the $36 range. When the global economy is once again churning full throttle, oil prices will likely spike again. Such volatility makes it difficult to predict the cost of shipping goods from China - and businesses hate uncertainty.

Admittedly, there are studies that question the impact of higher oil prices on China exports. One such study came to the conclusion that due to the large reserves of manufacturing workers in China, higher oil prices would affect China far less than its competitors.[27] However, since that report was written, China's demographic changes have soaked up those labor reserves, undercutting the author's main argument.

Simple common sense tells us that the price of goods manufactured in China that must first move from a factory to a port and then are transferred onto massive cargo ships that traverse the Pacific before being trucked to their final destination will be affected by oil price spikes. And as more and more China factories move inland and away from the coast, the impact will increase. Granted, higher oil prices alone will not be enough to undercut China's price advantage over US manufacturers. But it is another chink in the armor of the China manufacturing juggernaut.

Air Raid
The Pollution Problem

Recently, a Beijing artist, Liang Kegang, returned from a trip to Provence in southern France with a souvenir that he hoped to sell at auction as a piece of performance art. It was a hermetically sealed glass jar of air. The jar held three labels: one was the name of the town, Forcalquier, where the container was sealed; the second read "Air in Provence, France"; and the third bore his signature. The jar of air was purchased by an entrepreneur for $860.[28]

In 2007, a World Bank study estimated that only 1 percent of China's urban population of 560 million breathes air considered safe by the European Union. And 17 to 36 percent of air pollutants in China were generated by companies producing goods for export.[29] A February 2013 survey noted that breathing the air in Beijing was like smoking a pack of cigarettes a day. And what was the fashion statement on runways during Beijing's Fashion Week in November 2014? Designer smog masks.[30]

Airborne pollution is also having a significant effect on groundwater and the land itself. In April 2014, China's Ministry of Environmental Protection and Ministry of Land Resources issued a joint report stating that fully 20 percent of China's arable land is now so polluted that it is virtually off-limits to agriculture. The report cited "human industrial and agricultural activities" as the cause, with arsenic, cadmium, and nickel being the most prevalent pollutants.[31] This will have ominous consequences down the road for a country that must feed over 1.3 billion people.

For the last two decades, the Chinese government, driven by its chronic fear of social unrest, has been reluctant to address the severity of the pollution problem in order to keep factories open and workers employed. As recently as March 2015, the Communist Party cracked down on the distribution of a documentary video, "Under the Dome," that highlighted the severity of China's toxic air. The documentary, produced by a former Chinese journalist for state broadcaster China Central Television, was abruptly pulled from major video sites because authorities wanted to control "the online mood" during China's annual parliamentary meeting.[32] But as Liang's story illustrates, the severity of the pollution problem in China is now generating its own brand of unrest, and the government is likely to tighten regulations on factories in industries that are the source of the problem. The number of pollution cases heard before Chinese courts increased more than eightfold from 2013 to 2014, and noncompliant companies will face higher fines and increasing costs to become compliant.[33]

Ironically, the same study that calculated the amount of air pollutants generated by China companies manufacturing goods for export also found that large quantities of those pollutants are now finding their way across the Pacific Ocean to the US West Coast. When we offshore the production of goods to China, we import not only the products, but the resulting pollution as well.

Land Grab
Real Estate Speculation and Rising Manufacturing Costs

Finally, the bursting of the real estate bubble in China will also put further upward pressure on the price of goods manufactured there. What's the connection? A Chinese friend of mine, trained in economics, tells me that during the China real estate boom, manufacturers were leveraging the rising price of land to pad their bottom lines. While manufacturing goods in their factories for export, many of these companies were also involved in land speculation, buying land at favorable prices from the local government and then reselling it at a healthy profit to residential developers. There was so much money to be made in real estate that the land speculation tail began to wag the manufacturing dog. Large companies such as Haier and HiSense were making more money in real estate speculation than they were in manufacturing.

According to the China Real Estate Information Office, total real estate sales revenue in 2014 was down 75 percent from the same period in 2013. From April through September 2014, 20 percent of the land plots offered for sale by local governments went unsold. In the third quarter of 2014, the volume of land sales fell 47 percent compared to 2013.[34] Meanwhile, potential buyers are waiting for local governments to drop prices, while local governments wait for a People's Bank of China stimulus program to free up capital for potential buyers. The stalemate is likely to continue.

Now that real estate values are declining and exorbitant profits from the real estate boom have evaporated, those companies that had been subsidizing the manufacturing side of their business with profits from real estate will be forced to increase the prices of their manufactured goods to remain solvent.

Long Distance Runaround
Geography Matters

The Barton Company in Ohio buys printed dye sublimation[35] paper from one of my clients, Trans-Tex, and then heat transfers the designs from the paper onto narrow web fabric imported from China. In August 2012, Barton called and asked to buy surplus webbing inventory from Trans-Tex's domestic source because a typhoon had delayed their shipment from China. Years ago, they would have purchased enough inventory to ensure against such delays, but large inventory positions are costly today, particularly considering that the imported webbing in question now costs 50 percent more than it did several years ago.

After the inexorably rising price of goods made in China, geographic distance from the US market is the second inherent weakness in the China manufacturing model. This was much less of a problem in the 1980s and 90s when expected lead times were longer and US companies were willing to carry higher levels of inventory. However, in today's economy (and for the foreseeable future), the cash cycle is king, and demand for smaller inventory levels in a B2B environment, as well as on store shelves, requires speed to market. Given the increasing costs of transportation and the long lead times for ocean transport, speed to market requires proximity to market.

Top executives at companies interviewed in the litany of media reports on companies reshoring manufacturing to the United States almost unanimously mention the importance of geographic proximity to the US market as a critical factor in their supply chain strategy. Of course, distance from the US market is one of the weaknesses in the overseas manufacturing business model that cannot be overcome. China factories cannot change their geographic distance from their US customer base—although they can and do respond by either buying or building US factories.

Geographic distance becomes an even greater problem when a US customer revises an order with a short lead time or when there is a problem with faulty product and replacements must be delivered quickly. Under such challenging circumstances, communicating with a China vendor can be challenging at best and disastrous at worst.

Jacob Yount lived and worked in China for several years, has repatriated, and now writes a blog on the challenges of importing products from China. Yount has memorably described a Chinese factory as "a lumbering, destructive steamroller" that, once started, does not stop to ask for clarification on orders in process. If the China source faces questions during the manufacturing process, the default position will be a decision "that saves (the China factory) cost, time, material, energy, whatever, but to their advantage."[36] Yount goes on to detail the various parties that order revisions from the US customer must pass through, including the China sales office, the trading company, the production line, the cutting line, and the packing line, not to mention third-party vendors that may be part of the production process. Given the time zone differences and language barriers, stopping the lumbering steamroller, making changes, and then restarting that big machine costs a significant amount of time and money, particularly when the default position is to the cost benefit of the China source.

Clearly, given the need for speed to market and the demand for lower inventories, geographic distance creates another high hurdle for the traditional overseas manufacturing business model and adds to the cost of goods imported into the United States.

Junk Sale
US Regulations—and Bad Publicity—Are Changing the Game

Around 2000, GM was in a tight spot. Their profit margins were squeezed, and they were losing market share. GM's response? Cut costs. Their parts suppliers were urged to match what they called "the China cost," considered to be the lowest price possible using cheap China labor.[37] If the suppliers could not match those prices, they were told that the orders would be offshored. A loose spring in the ignition switch allowed their parts supplier to shave pennies off the price of the part, but it was ultimately linked to thirteen deaths and led to the recall of 1.6 million vehicles in 2014.

Two decades ago, the reaction of US manufacturers to the onslaught of overseas imports was to try to match the cost of the import. If it required cutting corners to do so, then corners were cut, and quality—and sometimes even safety—was sacrificed. US consumers were similarly focused almost exclusively on price. It's no accident that the Walmart slogan "Always the low price" debuted in the 1980s, just as the onslaught of low-priced imports was gaining steam. In that environment, China manufacturers, in general, paid little attention to product quality or safety. Why should they?

However, new and more rigorous consumer product safety regulations have altered the landscape. California Proposition 65 and the Consumer Products Safety Improvement Act (CPSIA) have raised the product safety bar, forcing manufacturers that want to sell into the US market to comply by changing base chemicals, parts, and production methods.

As product safety regulations have become more rigorous, high-profile stories such as the Tazreen factory fire and the Rana Plaza building collapse in Bangladesh have forced US importers to hold their overseas supply chains to higher standards than they have in the past. Fearing publicity that will reflect poorly on their brands, big-box retailers and international brands have become far more sensitive to wages and working conditions in their supply chains. This has sharply curtailed the ability of China factories making brand-name consumer goods to underpay workers or subcontract work to lower-cost local factories with dangerous working conditions or abusively low pay.

The mainstream media—and social media in particular—have also kept the questionable quality of manufactured goods from China constantly in the public eye. A litany of stories, including numerous product recalls, the collapse of poorly constructed apartment buildings in Shanghai, faulty pipes leaking oil into the drinking water of Lanzhou (population two point four million), and defective steel rods from China used in the rebuilding of the Oakland Bay bridge, continues to focus a spotlight on the general lack of a quality culture in the China manufacturing community.

And while it's true that US companies buy from China when they want cheaper, it's equally true that China companies buy from the United States when they want higher quality. Vibco Vibrators, based in Wyoming,

Rhode Island, is a prime manufacturer of industrial vibrators, used for the compaction and handling of bulk materials. Industrial vibrators are used in over 615 industries from mining to pharmaceuticals. When China was building the world's largest hydroelectric power project over the Yangtze River and they needed industrial vibrators, they didn't buy them from a China manufacturer; they bought them from Vibco.

The bottom line is that overseas manufacturers will now be forced to bear the higher costs of compliance with more rigorous US product safety regulations at the same time that increased supply chain scrutiny is making it more difficult for them to lower costs by cutting production corners or endangering the health and safety of their workers. Higher costs mean shrinking margins for those manufacturers and higher prices for US importers on finished goods and parts coming into the United States from overseas.

Let's Shake on It
The Trust Factor

Recently, a friend and I were discussing the challenges of working with a China manufacturer, and he recalled an incident that occurred when he was with Texas Instruments roughly twenty-five years ago. The company was having a part made in China that they had designed specifically for a particular product. About six months after their new product launched, they discovered that their part was being used in a knockoff that was also manufactured in China. Amazingly, the Chinese parts supplier had not even bothered to remove the Texas Instruments branding from the part before selling it to the knockoff manufacturer.

There is one major weakness in the overseas manufacturing business model that has very little to do with the actual cost of the product. Can you trust your overseas source? Will they pirate your ideas? An extensive 2013 report from the National Bureau of Asian Research found that 50 to 80 percent of international intellectual property theft cases involved China. The report also noted that while China continues to pass stiffer laws against IP property theft, national industrial policy goals actually encourage it.[38]

Several years ago, the Federal Trade Commission in Canada released this laundry list of examples of China IP theft:

Example 1
Someone registers your trademark. Yes, that is exactly how it sounds. You can no longer use your name in China. Not too much you can do about it, either, except to scrap all that marketing material you just printed.

Example 2
Someone has copied your website—word for word, photo for photo. Think your existing clients can tell the difference?

Example 3
Your local partner loves your company's offering so much that they decide to go it alone, becoming your newest competitor and worst nightmare, offering your products and using your client list.

Of course, there is also the classic case of the US importer who discovers that his China source is now selling to his US customer. This could be either a conscious strategy on the part of the China source or the bumbling mistake of an overseas company that does not fully understand the nature of the distribution network here in the United States. In either case, you could suddenly find yourself losing customers because your overseas source is selling to your customer at exactly the same price (or lower) than they sell to you. It's difficult to get that business back—but not as difficult as it was ten or twenty years ago.

In the spring of 2013, Tramontina USA, a manufacturer of cookware with headquarters based in Sugar Land, Texas, announced that it was expanding production at its Wisconsin facility to satisfy a burgeoning demand for a wider range of colors in its line. In a press release, the president and CEO of Tramontina, Antonio Galafassi, explained that they had "seen tremendous growth and opportunity both with retailers who want to carry quality 'Made in the USA' products at competitive pricing and with consumers, who more than ever, are wanting to buy domestic-made products." Cited as the advantages to domestic production were (1) the ability to manufacture lower minimum quantities, (2) speed to market, and (3) superior quality control.[39]

As I read stories like this one over the course of the last five years, I noticed that the common denominator for most of them was the three advantages just listed. Almost every company that was reshoring production to the United States—or winning business back from overseas competitors—mentioned some variation on this theme when explaining their decision. This is no coincidence. Shipping small minimum-order sizes is a problem for overseas manufacturers, given their traditional focus on long production runs and the necessity of shipping larger orders to minimize freight costs. As for speed to market, they are half a world away and can only overcome geography by asking the customer to bear the cost of expedited shipping methods. And neither quality nor compliance to product safety standards has historically been a core competency of Pacific Rim manufacturers, particularly those in China. Their focus has been almost exclusively on providing the lowest possible price.

Clearly these three advantages strike at the greatest vulnerabilities in the China manufacturing business model. If US consumers and B2B buyers want to place smaller or more customized orders, if they want what they ordered to be delivered tomorrow (not two weeks or two months from now), and if they want better quality and safer products, then China manufacturers are vulnerable.

These anecdotal success stories only confirmed a strategy that I had deduced while navigating Trans-Tex through the depths of the Great Recession. We concentrated on the three core principles of *fewer, faster,* and *finer* and managed to generate double-digit sales increases each year while competing directly with China manufacturers. We were not in a high-tech, high-innovation, or "advanced" industry; we were in a very basic industry that involved a great deal of hand assembly work. Initially, I thought that perhaps we were successful because of a quirk in our distribution network or because we were in a niche market. But as I read more and more stories—from a wide range of industries—about companies successfully competing against imports, company spokespeople would always cite at least two of these principles and often all three.

So if these principles are so effective, why has it taken us twenty-five years and the loss of six million manufacturing jobs to figure it out? We have been slow to realize that the US customer, indeed the global customer, has changed over the past two decades; and those changes are breaking to the advantage of small to midsize US manufacturers. I once believed—even preached—that we would never reshore a significant number of manufacturing jobs. When I first battled China manufacturers twenty-five years ago, the price gap with China was gaping, cheap was more important than unique, expected production lead times were significantly longer, there was no Consumer Products Safety Improvement Act, and intellectual property theft by China manufacturers had not yet become epidemic.

Now the price gap with China is narrowing dramatically, customers want what they want when they want it, and they are increasingly leery of unsafe, poorly made products. And B2B buyers here in the United States are much more aware of the possibility of intellectual property theft and the ability of a China manufacturer to bypass them and sell directly to the ultimate customer. All of these factors have opened a window of opportunity for quick, nimble US manufacturers to utilize the principles of *fewer, faster,* and *finer* to exploit these weaknesses in the China manufacturing business model.

As noted previously, we lost over six million manufacturing jobs over the course of the last twenty-five years. It has been estimated that approximately half of those went to China. This book is about how to get those jobs back. But let's first review how we put ourselves in this predicament.

CHAPTER 2

The Tale of Two Companies—Living in the Best and Worst of Times

> In any military operation, it is important first
> to know the lay of the land.[40]
> *The Art of War*

Offshoring was death by a thousand cuts, but we tend to think of it in the aggregate as though one giant sword of Damocles pared through our manufacturing base. The number of lost jobs is so staggering, perhaps the only way to fathom its magnitude is to think of it as one cataclysmic event.

But thinking of offshoring in this way also leads us to forget that hundreds of particular industries and literally thousands of small to midsize companies here in the United States were slowly strangled to death. Offshoring wasn't just an execution; for many small manufacturing companies, it was a long death march that concluded in an execution. For example, most of us have forgotten that shoe manufacturing was once a thriving industry here. My wife's uncle, Frank Speroni, grew up in that business after his service in World War II and witnessed its apex, long decline, and ultimate demise. He still speaks fondly of the people he met in the shoe business and the experiences he enjoyed. But he almost always ends those stories with a wistful sigh because they remind him of a once-proud industry that slowly disappeared.

The following two brief histories are representative accounts of how manufacturing slipped away from our shores; they serve as reminders that offshoring is a story of individual people and companies. I understand Uncle Frank's emotions because I've shared his experience. I helped a very small company, the Quill Company[41], grow into a much bigger one; participated in the sweat and tears that eventually led to the satisfaction of success; and watched almost helplessly as offshoring slowly destroyed everything that we had built. And Quill's story is not much different from thousands of others in hundreds of other industries.

Just-A-Stretch was another small, family-owned Rhode Island company devastated by offshoring, but from a different industry—textiles. Although seemingly unrelated, these two companies' common thread is that key employees from both companies eventually came together and found a way to win round 2 in the battle against imports—*fewer, faster,* and *finer.* Some of the distribution network details may seem arcane or convoluted, but remember that the devil of offshoring has always been in the details.

The Write Stuff

In the choir loft of what was formerly a small wooden church, I was offered and accepted my first manufacturing job. The choir loft was the company's only meeting space. The church's main floor had been converted to manufacturing and held about a dozen tables used for assembly. The front of the choir loft had been walled off from the main factory floor to muffle the noise of assembly machines. Across a small parking lot with six spaces was the two-story tenement that held what would be my first office.

My desk was in the first-floor kitchen. The old sink was a few feet from my desk. The kitchen had one of those old ironing boards on a hinge that tucked into a small cabinet cut into the wall. I used the kitchen cupboards as my filing cabinet. The company's receptionist and her husband lived in an apartment on the top floor. The ground floor was offices, and the dirt-floor basement was used to store files. Connected to the tenement through a basement hallway was a small stone building that housed a second small assembly area and a shipping department. It was 1981. I knew little about manufacturing and nothing about battling imports.

A chance encounter led to the job. Immediately after college in the late 1970s, I was employed as an assistant buyer at a large retail chain with outlets throughout the Northeast. One of the senior merchandise managers was retiring, and the buying staff was attending a farewell reception at a local hotel. At the party, the buyer for whom I worked introduced me to her husband, and the next day he called and asked if I would like to come and work for him. He was one of the second-generation owners of a small pen manufacturing company, the Quill Company, based in Providence, Rhode Island. At the time, the company had fewer than twenty employees, including the four family members who ran the business. Their sales and marketing manager was on the verge of retirement, and the family owners were looking to hire a young person who could learn the business and eventually replace the retiring executive.

The company began as a pen mechanism manufacturer, T&T (Tessier & Tessier), in 1949. Founded by Aram Tessier to provide twist mechanisms to other pen manufacturers, T&T bought the rights to the Quill brand in 1972. Already owning the patent on their own twist pen mechanism, it was relatively easy for T&T to enter the finished goods business by simply buying the cap, barrel, and clip assemblies needed to build a pen from other local manufacturers.

Quill marketed its writing instruments primarily to the promotional products market. What are promotional products? Some people now call them "swag," and some still call them advertising specialties. Look around your home, office, or car, and you're likely to see some. Do you have a pen or coffee mug on your desk? There is a good chance that the pen or mug has a company name or logo printed on it. Maybe there is a plaque on your wall given to you as a memento for a job well done. Perhaps there is a sticky notepad with your company name on it and motivational phrases that get you through the day. You may even have a printed calendar on your wall, given to you by your office supply dealer or your local church. You likely remember who gave it to you because the organization or company had their name printed on it. The tote bag you use to carry your lunch to work? It probably has the name of a company printed on it as well. All of these are promotional products.

In a nutshell, promotional products are items that are imprinted with an advertiser's logo and distributed, usually for free, to customers and/

or potential customers. According to Promotional Products Association International (PPAI), the industry's trade association, one of the first-known promotional products was a campaign button distributed when George Washington was running for president. Since then, everything from coffee mugs to pens to calendars to key tags to coasters to mouse pads have been imprinted with logos or slogans and handed out by companies to advertise their brand to a target audience.

The father of the modern promotional products business was Jasper Meeks, a newspaper publisher in Coshocton, Ohio, who was simply looking for a way to keep his printing presses busy. One day he saw some schoolchildren struggling to carry their books home from school and came up with the idea of selling burlap bags to a local shoe store with the store's name, Cantwell Shoes, printed on the side. The bags would then be given to children to haul their books to and from school, spreading his ad all over town.[42] Some of the earliest promotional products of this era included wall calendars, yardsticks, horse blankets, cloth caps, aprons, and hand fans.[43]

The ubiquity of promotional products is reflected in the size of the marketplace, $20 billion in 2014.[44] As a basis for comparison, the total box office gross receipts for movie ticket sales in the same year were roughly $10.4 billion. Because they are distributed directly to each individual recipient, promotional products are often considered the most highly targeted form of advertising, making them the most cost-effective vehicle for conveying an advertising message.

For decades, the marketplace for the distribution of promotional products was remarkably insular. Advertisers would buy the products from a highly fragmented network of promotional products distributors. These local distribution companies were and are, on average, quite small; forty-five years ago, one third were one-person companies operating out of their homes. In the late 1970s, 74 percent of the 3,700 listed distributor companies reported yearly sales of less than $200,000; 50 percent reported sales of less than $100,000.[45] The distributors would sell the products to an advertiser and then forward an order and the advertiser's artwork to the supplier/manufacturer. Suppliers, most of which were small US manufacturers, would imprint (or decorate) their product with the logo, then ship the order directly to the advertiser. The supplier would then invoice the distributor, who in turn invoiced the advertiser. This allowed both the supplier and distributor to average roughly a 40 percent margin on each sale.

One might ask why the advertiser, in order to buy at a lower price, would not simply bypass the distributor company and buy the product directly from the supplier/manufacturer. The answer is that such a transaction would violate the industry protocol, which had evolved over decades. Supplier/manufacturers generally would sell only through the established network because the distributor functioned as the sales force for the supplier. Given that supplier companies, like distributors, were relatively small, they could not afford to hire a sales force that would cover the entire country. Distributor companies, largely local, served that purpose. If the distributors were to get wind that a supplier company was bypassing them and selling directly to the advertiser, it is unlikely that they would continue to push that particular supplier's products.

Distributor companies in the promotional products market generally held (and still hold) sway because they own the relationship with the advertiser. It was the distributor salesperson who recommended a particular product to the advertiser, and it was through those product recommendations that distributors could steer business to those supplier/manufacturers they favored. However, the distributor salesperson provided more than simply a sourcing service; they also counseled the advertiser as to the best product to use for a particular advertising effort, what message should be printed on the product, and how the product should be distributed to the target audience.

Quill was a supplier/manufacturer. The most complicated aspect of the business for suppliers like Quill was customizing each product with an advertising message. Typically, these orders were event-driven; that is, they were ordered for a specific event that took place at a specific time (e.g., company picnic, trade show giveaway, grand opening). If the order was not correctly imprinted with the advertiser's logo or slogan and shipped to arrive before the event, the product was virtually useless. Thus, much care was taken to ensure that the advertising copy was correct and that it was printed exactly as the advertiser desired (proper colors, imprint centered, correct spelling, etc.).[46] Such attention to detail requires a great deal of communication among advertiser, distributor, and supplier, adding to the cost of producing the order.

Whereas this cost is easily amortized in a large order, the overwhelming majority of orders are very small. Average industry order size for a distributor has hovered between $600 and $1,000 for the last forty-five years. Given that distributors typically sell products at a 35 to 40 percent gross margin, the corresponding average order size for suppliers was $360 to $600.

If the bread and butter of the business was the average-size order, the gravy was the long production run. Occasionally, a large advertiser such as AT&T, Ford, American Airlines, or Coca-Cola would need promotional products for a new product launch or employee giveaway. Distributors would compete aggressively to get this business, and then bid it out to multiple suppliers, who would shave margins to secure the order. Although the profit on such business was much lower than on the typical industry order, the long production run covered a significant degree of the supplier's yearly overhead and smoothed out the peaks and valleys of the business cycle. A supplier able to nab only two or three of these orders each year could ensure a healthy bottom line.

Then there is the factor of lead time. Promotional products are often one of the last components considered when a promotional campaign is developed by the advertiser. Last-minute buying decisions, for quantities large and small, are not unusual. Thus, suppliers are forced to compete not only on product, price, and imprint quality, but turnaround time as well. From the '60s through the '80s, average lead times, depending on the product and imprinting method, were three to four weeks.[47] It was not uncommon for distributors to receive last-minute requests from advertisers for custom imprinted product to be produced and shipped within a couple of weeks. At Quill, our standard production lead time in 1981 for pens decorated with a corporate logo was six to twelve weeks.

The production lead time at Quill was higher than the industry average due to the decorating method used. At the time, the standard Quill ballpoint pen looked very much like the traditional A. T. Cross pen that had been the gift given to millions of high school and college graduates during the middle decades of the last century. Those pens, like most others in the promotional products business, were imprinted with a corporate logo by affixing a metal emblem to the pen's clip. These emblems were created either through a metal die-striking process or by laying screened colors on a flat metal background. The quality level was high, but the lead time was daunting—four to six weeks to produce a silk-screen emblem and eight to ten weeks to produce a die-struck emblem. Also, the process was costly, adding anywhere from $1.25 to $2.50 to the distributor's cost. This would translate to roughly $2.00 to $4.00 additional cost to the advertiser, in addition to the longer production lead time.

In 1981, shortly after I came on board, Quill introduced a new pen with a slant top. This new product design lent itself ideally to the promotional products market. Just drop a company logo into the slant-top area, and you had a quality pen that perfectly presented the advertiser's logo when the pen was sitting in a shirt or jacket pocket or held in a writing position. Instead of going to the expense and long lead time of outsourcing the manufacture of a metal emblem, Quill created a full-color photographic representation of the advertiser's logo, applied a clear epoxy dome for protection, and glued the domed piece to the slant top of the pen. This process could be done on-site at the Quill factory more quickly and for a much lower cost than the metal emblem traditionally attached to the clip. Also, precisely because the process was photographic, any number of colors could be reproduced.

A similar imprinting method had been pioneered by the Garland Pen Company, also based in Rhode Island. Quill's innovation was to take what had been Garland's flat top and cut the cap of the pen at an angle, creating a slant top on the pen that maximized the exposure of the advertiser's logo. The pricing strategy at Quill, similar to Garland's, was to roll up the relatively low cost of the "photo logo" into the cost of the pen, eliminating extra charges to the distributor and, by extension, to the advertiser. A unique, new promotional pen had been created, which could be customized with an advertiser's logo in any number of colors for no additional charge (saving the advertiser $2.00 to $4.00 per pen) and was deliverable in ten working days or less.

This reduction in Quill's lead time (remember that most promotional products were being produced in two to four weeks) dovetailed exactly with the industry's movement toward increasingly shorter lead times during the second half of the 1980s and early 1990s. Bottom line, the promotional products network needed to produce hundreds of thousands of $500 orders for customized products in four weeks or less. This need for the combination of speed, product quality, and imprint accuracy justified the relatively healthy margins in the industry through the 1980s.

Sales of this newly designed slant-top pen quickly accelerated, primarily due to the lower cost of decorating the pen with a logo and the relatively speedy production lead time. With sales booming in the United States, our next frontier was the international marketplace. We found distribution partners in Canada, Mexico, and Europe. We hired sales agents in Singapore, Malaysia, Australia, South Africa, and Hong Kong. Each year I would attend the Hong Kong Premium & Gift Fair to conduct a sales meeting with our Pacific Rim distributors. As I recall, at that time Quill was the only US-based promotional products manufacturer pioneering sales efforts in Canada, Mexico, Europe, and Asia. While other US companies were beginning to source imported products from China, our goal was to export to China.

By the early 1990s, with Quill's business booming both domestically and internationally, we had outgrown the small complex of buildings in the Olneyville section of Providence and made plans to build a new manufacturing facility in Cranston, Rhode Island. What had been, in 1979, a small pen mechanism manufacturer housed in a rickety wooden converted church was, by 1994, one of the most widely recognized writing instrument brands in the promotional products market, with 120 employees housed in a brand-new 45,000-square-foot facility just off Interstate 295 in Cranston, Rhode Island.

Shortly after moving to the new facility, *Consumer Reports* magazine rated a Quill writing instrument best of class in its category. It marked the first time that Quill received recognition in a national retail publication and cemented the company's reputation for quality.

In the spring of 2000, I was invited to Washington, DC, to address a subcommittee of the US Senate's Committee on Foreign Relations. Lincoln Chafee, who had just been appointed to the Senate to fill out the term of his recently departed father, John Chafee, was the chair of the Subcommittee on Western Hemisphere, Peace Corps, Narcotics, and Terrorism. Through a contact at the Rhode Island Economic Development Corporation, I was asked to testify on the effects of the North American Free Trade Agreement. As a confirmed internationalist, my testimony was bullish on free trade and NAFTA. I argued that NAFTA had not gone far enough in minimizing the friction in cross border trade with Canada and Mexico and encouraged committee members to continue to pursue trade deals with other parts of the world.

It was a position I would come to regret. But at the time, my focus was on the offensive side of the ball, attempting to spur sales in overseas markets. Meanwhile, I missed what was slowly happening on defense, in the US market. When cheap pens made by China manufacturers first began pouring in, our growth was still steady at Quill. My biggest mistake was assuming that our continuing growth meant that we were adequately competing with the imports when, in fact, we were still benefiting from the overall growth of the marketplace. I didn't realize that the best of times sometimes overlap with the worst of times.

As the new millennium approached, the promotional products industry, Quill, and my career were all riding high. But the 1990s were the high-water mark for the traditional promotional products distribution network and for US promotional products suppliers, like Quill, that were domestic manufacturers, because the same macroeconomic forces that led to China outsourcing in so many other US industries finally caught up with promotional products.

Too Much Information

In 1995, while vice president of international sales and marketing at Quill, I received a letter from the president of one of the twenty-five largest distributor companies in the promotional products business. He spent the first half of the letter denigrating supplier companies that had created websites, branding them as suppliers who were trying to "sell direct" and bypass the distributor network. The second half of the letter was a warning that if Quill launched a website, his company would no longer do business with us.

In retrospect, the letter seems a laughable anachronism. Today, virtually every company has a website. And ironically enough, sales tailed off at this distributor company that was strong-arming suppliers in an attempt to prevent them from launching websites, and it eventually became an acquisition target. But this executive's concern, although misdirected, was well-founded.

Keep in mind that the promotional products distribution network was built on the feasibility of hiding information. Advertisers who bought promotional products did not know the manufacturing source of the product or the markup between the supplier/decorator and the distributor. Supplier catalogs, as previously noted, bore no information (address, phone number, company name) that would allow the advertiser to identify and track down the manufacturer. In order to help assuage distributor concerns about being bypassed, most suppliers created a brand name for their product line that differed from their actual company name to make it more difficult for advertisers to find them. Distributor owners at the time even prevented their salespeople from contacting suppliers directly. The entire supply chain had been constructed to ensure maximum opacity.

Websites were a game changer. What most concerned this particular distributor principal was that if suppliers had websites, then advertisers would be able to find them with the click of a mouse and attempt to buy directly from the supplier. He understood that knowledge became buying power. And although he was correct about how the Internet would break down the industry's antiquated information barriers, he was wrong about the parties best poised to take advantage of the new informational landscape. They would not be US manufacturers like Quill, who remained loyal to the traditional US distribution network, but manufacturers in China.

Consider the Source

Between 1970 and 1990, during the halcyon days of the traditional network for US-based promotional products manufacturers, supplier companies could be identified by their product category. For example, Quill was a pen company, Hazel was a portfolio company, Worldwide was a coffee mug company, and Advertising Unlimited was a calendar company. Thus, a supplier company was known chiefly by the type of product it manufactured and imprinted. Product lines were narrow, with relatively few models, and deep, with a robust inventory of those models.

As the manufacturing of commodity products such as pens, key tags, and coffee mugs moved increasingly to China, US companies that were historically prime manufacturers experienced declining sales in their core product category and began to augment their lines with imported product. Because the primary value added by a US promotional products supplier was printing the advertiser's logo on a product, it began to matter less and less whether that product was manufactured in the United States or abroad.

A US company manufacturing canvas bags for the promotional products market could begin to source other products (coffee mugs, key tags, pens, coasters) in China, put them on a shelf in their warehouse, market them to distributors, and imprint them with the advertiser's logo on receipt of an order. Since these supplier companies already had an established sales network through the local distributor companies, they could easily expand their product offering and increase their top line by *importing* these ancillary products and acting as more of a decorator (or imprinter) than as a manufacturer.

The ever smaller world of global sourcing facilitated this process. What were once domestic companies involved in light manufacturing slowly morphed into importer/decorators. Although this was a quick and painless way to expand a product line, the Achilles heel of this strategy was that, compared to manufacturing, there was little or no barrier to entry. If a US supplier was importing the hottest coffee mug in the industry from a source in China, its competitor could source that mug from the same China manufacturer, and begin marketing it to the US distributor base in a matter of months, if not weeks.

The costs for tooling and molds, particularly in China, were dramatically lower than those same costs domestically. Due to the lower development costs overseas, new product designs rolled out of China at an increasingly rapid clip. Just as quickly as they were developed and imported into the United States, the designs were copied and imported by competing suppliers. This allowed distributor companies to price the same product from competing domestic suppliers, playing one against the other and driving down supplier margins.

It also had the effect of more quickly churning the product life cycles in the promotional products industry. If one could simply import and warehouse plain goods for imprinting, there were no manufacturing development costs. Instead of creating new and innovative proprietary products, supplier companies developed new lines by making shopping trips to trade fairs in China.

At Quill, as early as 1990, we began to feel the effects of this seismic shift in the landscape. Instead of competing against established retail pen brands such as A. T. Cross, Parker, and Sheaffer, we noticed that we were increasingly competing against upstart supplier companies importing pens off the shelf from any one of a number of low-cost Asian manufacturers. These generic pens were half the price of Quill products. Although not the same quality, the designs were innovative, sporting large imprint areas to maximize the capacity for advertising copy. One manufacturer in China made a much cheaper, identical copy of the slant-top Quill pen and began selling it into the United States, and we were forced to spend tens of thousands of dollars to protect our design patent.

In the 1980s, we at Quill were able to sell against these low-priced imports by stressing the significant difference in quality and that our product was US-made. However, year by year, the quality difference narrowed, while the pricing difference remained. Even more alarmingly, advertisers who bought the products were becoming less influenced by the "Made in the U.S.A." label and Quill's lifetime guarantee. They might express a bias toward product that was domestically manufactured, but if the pricing gap was wide—and the order large enough—the advertiser's budget took precedence.

Within the space of a few short years, the multiproduct importer/decorators were the only growing supplier companies in the promotional products marketplace. Instead of product-centric manufacturing companies, the US supplier marketplace quickly became dominated by companies that either began as importer/decorators or morphed into one after having seen the writing on the wall. Those US-based manufacturing companies unable to react to this shift in the business model were increasingly marginalized.

Quill was one of them. By the turn of the millennium, the company was gamely struggling to compete, attempting to straddle the fence between pen manufacturer and pen importer. Lacking a highly recognized retail brand name, it was difficult in the promotional products market to command the higher price points driven by domestic manufacturing. Lacking overseas sourcing and importing expertise, Quill was increasingly beaten by the price-driven importer/decorators. On the product development side, they could not keep pace with the explosive, but brief, product life cycles that had become typical in the industry.

Remember that it was far easier to change your product line quickly if you were simply importing products from an Asian manufacturer, as opposed to the extensive tooling costs a US manufacturer like Quill would need to invest to launch a new line. Also, the Asian manufacturers could amortize their tooling costs over multiple customers because they weren't selling a branded product—they were selling a commodity. Reluctant to stray from the company's core competency as a prime manufacturer of writing instruments and its traditional identity, Quill never broadened their line to include commodity-type products imported from China manufacturers, a strategy that had proven successful for several other single-product line suppliers.

Simply put, traditional US promotional products supplier/manufacturers could not compete with the lower product development and manufacturing costs in China. Within the space of a decade, most US suppliers were either transitioning to the importer/decorator model or had fully implemented the strategy. Those supplier companies that started during this global transition and created a business model based solely on importing and decorating (vs. manufacturing and decorating) were the most successful and have remained so. Today, over 95 percent of promotional products distributed in the United States are manufactured overseas.

Although the importer/decorator model was the most effective strategy for growth during the 1990s and at the beginning of the new millennium, there was an inherent weakness in the longer-term strategy. What if those overseas sources that manufactured such inexpensive commodity products learned to imprint corporate logos on those products? And what if they used the power of the Internet to market their manufacturing and decorating capabilities directly to the distributors and/or advertisers? To put it another way, if an advertiser could source the complete imprinted order for a far lower price overseas, why use the traditional distribution network? Why not simply order promotional products—particularly the larger orders—directly from the overseas source? Given that the information needed to locate that source was now readily available on the Internet; given that lower-priced, expedited shipping methods on smaller orders were now being touted by freight companies; and given that production lead times out of China were increasingly faster, what value did the traditional US supplier company add to the supply chain?

Not with a Bang …

In 2002, after nineteen years with Quill and two subsequent years with a technology company, I founded International Marketing Advantages, a small firm specializing in marketing consulting and mergers and acquisitions. Through a combination of my experience with Quill and observing the sea change in the marketplace during the '90s, I had developed very specific ideas about what was happening to the traditional distribution network of suppliers and distributors and about where the industry was headed.

As the new millennium dawned, it was clear that larger orders would continue to be shopped directly overseas by both distributors and advertisers. China manufacturers were learning to decorate and market directly to advertisers here in the United States, skimming off the larger orders from Fortune 500 advertisers (e.g., 25,000 coffee mugs, 50,000 caps). Remember that these larger orders had traditionally been an important factor in the healthy bottom lines of US supplier/manufacturers back in the 1970s and 1980s. Given the continuing loss of larger orders to China, US suppliers have now been forced to cut margins to maintain the midsize order business at the same time that their internal costs for processing each order are increasing. Bottom line, if a supplier company cannot make money on a $500 customized order in the new global environment, it will not survive. And many haven't.

Secondly, with the average dollar size of each customized order continuing its downward trend and increasing pressure on lead times, operational excellence is becoming increasingly essential if US supplier companies are to remain profitable. Average lead times had shrunk from six to twelve weeks to three to five days over the course of thirty years. Many suppliers are now offering twenty-four-hour service. This is primarily possible because the products are imported, placed on a warehouse shelf, and decorated overnight.

Supplier business models are also evolving to cope with the reality of globalization. Some China manufacturers are now selling through US-based agents who act as importers of imprinted goods, supplanting the role of the traditional US supplier company. Piggybacking on the concept, a new US-based model has developed of "supplier" companies that neither warehouse nor decorate promotional products. They market to distributor companies through advertising in the trade press and attending trade shows, but send the resulting orders to factories in China, from which the product is shipped directly to either the distributor or advertiser. Asian sourcing companies have opened offices in the United States and are now selling directly to both distributors and advertisers, bypassing even the US importer/decorator. And most ominously, China manufacturers that once provided blank product to US supplier importers are now starting up their own factories in the United States to warehouse and imprint their products and sell them directly to the distributor customers of the US suppliers they have bypassed.

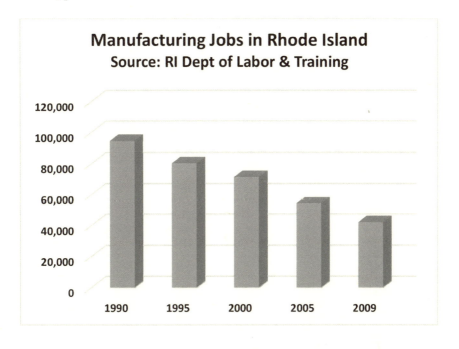

Thus, although US promotional products manufacturers were the first to succumb to the changes in the marketplace, even importing suppliers and distributors are now under increasing margin pressure due to direct sales into the United States from China. It is a precarious scenario for these companies—lower average order size, decreasing margins, and increasing sales volume bypassing them and going directly from China manufacturer/decorators to advertisers.

Meanwhile, after 2000, sales at Quill, one of the success stories of Rhode Island manufacturing in the last quarter of the twentieth century, had begun to slowly drift downward; it was death by a thousand cuts. In 2008, the company was sold to Newell Rubbermaid, moved to Janesville, Wisconsin, and folded into their Sanford Business-to-Business division along with Sharpie, Parker, and other pen brands. A press release from Sanford in mid-2009 announced that they were moving all of their pen operations, including Quill, to Mexico.

A Tangled Web

After arriving in the United States on his mission to bring textile manufacturing to the New World, Samuel Slater built his first factory along the banks of the Blackstone River in Pawtucket, Rhode Island, in 1793. Thus, the US textile industry remained centered in New England up to the middle of the twentieth century. In addition to the proliferation of mills in Rhode Island, others sprouted up in Lowell, Lawrence, and Fall River, Massachusetts. At the time, the rudimentary apparel supply chain included southern cotton farmers who sold their crop to northeastern mills that would convert the cotton into yarn. The yarn would then be made into fabric, and the fabric would go to a cut and sew operation to be transformed into a garment.

As costs slowly rose in the northeast, mills began migrating to the southeast to find a cheaper labor source and closer proximity to cotton supplies. Global competition put further downward pressure on manufacturing costs, and mills relocated farther south to Mexico and the Caribbean and, ultimately, to China. Between 1948 and 1995,

US employment in the textile industry dipped from 1.3 million jobs to approximately 650,000.[48]

Narrow webbing is a niche segment of the textile business that generally followed the migration of the mills. Narrow web fabrics are used in a wide variety of products, including strapping for bags, trim for apparel (think of the elastic used as a waistband for pants and undergarments for brand names such as Hanes and Jockey), shoelaces, men's suspenders, and trim on furniture or drapes. Many US webbing manufacturers, like their counterparts in the broader fabric business, shuttered their US operations during the second half of the twentieth century, moving to the Caribbean and Central America to better compete with imports from China. Sometimes the strategy worked; often it did not.

Just-A-Stretch, like so many others, died a slow death. A family-owned manufacturer of narrow webbing for the textile industry, the company was founded in 1975 by Robert Laferriere, Sr., in Hope, Rhode Island. Laferriere grew up in Rhode Island but eventually settled in Hagerstown, Maryland, to work for C. M. Offray and Son. Offray was one of the oldest ribbon companies in the United States, founded in 1876 by a French fabric designer who worked in the New York City area as a representative for a French ribbon manufacturer. In 1922, the company relocated its plant from New Jersey to Hagerstown and concentrated on making webbing for parachutes used by the military in World War II. Both Laferriere and his brother joined Offray in the late 1950s at the urging of their father, who worked there as well.

Laferriere was eventually courted away from Offray by the precursor company to Georgia Narrow Fabrics. Laferriere was hired to set up their new operation in Jessup, Georgia. An Italian company, Comez, had recently invented a new flatbed knitting machine that lowered the price of fabricating elastic webbing, and Georgia Narrow Fabrics wanted to take advantage of both the new technology and lower labor costs in the Southeast. Laferriere spent several years commuting from his home in Connecticut to the factory in Georgia.

In 1975, tired of the travel grind and time spent away from his young family, he mortgaged his house to buy knitting equipment, was loaned yarn by a longtime industry contact, and set up his own company, Just-A-Stretch, in West Warwick, Rhode Island. His first order of business was to make a cold call on Fruit of the Loom, at the time the largest US buyer of printed elastic webbing. Remarkably, his persistence paid off, and in a few short months Fruit of the Loom had become their largest customer and the cornerstone of his business. Twenty years later, the company's sales were topping $15 million, and Laferriere's knitting machines were humming, producing over 4.5 million yards of elastic per week. Fruit of the Loom represented 50 percent of their total sales.

Throughout the company's dramatic growth, Just-A-Stretch never had a late shipment and never had a return. Yet in 2000, Laferriere was contacted by Fruit of the Loom and abruptly informed that the elastic program would be put out for bid and that the lowest bidder would get the business. He put together an aggressive price and believed that years of providing excellent service and quality would give him an additional edge. But a vendor in the Southeast with a factory in El Salvador offered a lower price, and Fruit of the Loom pulled the program. With its business suddenly cut in half, Laferriere and his son, Bob, Jr., struggled to keep the company going. They were able to briefly stabilize the business by picking up another large customer, Delta Galil, which bought elastic trim printed with cartoon characters for children's apparel.

But the death spiral of Just-A-Stretch accelerated with China's entry into the World Trade Organization in December 2001. Tariffs on competing products from China dropped virtually overnight, and China manufacturers could now sell at significantly lower prices. This led to the loss of Delta Galil as a customer. Laferriere responded by opening up an operation in the Dominican Republic in order to take advantage of lower labor costs, but the downward spiral continued. Sales at Just-A-Stretch plunged from $10 million in 2003 to $3 million in 2005, as China competition picked off most of their midsize customers. Cut and sew operations were now migrating to China from the Caribbean basin, and it became more cost-effective for apparel brands to source webbing near the China assembly operations. Ultimately, other low-cost countries like Bangladesh, Vietnam, and Pakistan entered the textile business, sucking more jobs to Asia. The number of employees at Just-a-Stretch dropped from 110 to twenty. Although the Laferrieres continued to fight the good fight, they eventually were forced to close operations and merge into a consolidation of other downsized webbing manufacturers decimated by offshoring.

By the turn of the century, only a handful of narrow webbing manufacturers were still hanging on in Rhode Island, but they had downsized and were serving mostly niche markets, including Department of Defense contracts requiring US sourcing due to the Barry Amendment[49] and regulated markets such as the auto industry (e.g., seat belts). Some had moved production to Central America or the Caribbean and maintained only an office in the Northeast. Naturally, given the overseas migration of textile mills, if you were part of the domestic supply chain that supplied those mills, your company was living on borrowed time. Trans-Tex LLC was one of those companies.

CHAPTER 3

The Enemy Within—Extinguish the Fire

> Whether you live or die depends upon the
> configuration of the battleground.
> Whether you survive or perish depends on the way of battle.[50]
> *The Art of War*

If Quill and Just-A-Stretch are representative examples of the devastation of offshoring, how and why are they typical? What were the factors that led to their downfall, and who or what is to blame? Some might say that their demise was inevitable, that they were victims of economic and cultural forces beyond the control of those who managed the companies. To a certain degree, that's true. But to say that the massive offshoring of US manufacturing jobs happened solely due to factors beyond our control is a convenient way for those responsible to duck that responsibility. There is plenty of blame to pass around. Here are the main culprits:

1. Macroeconomic forces (yes, they did contribute)
2. Actions of individual companies
3. Government policies
4. Consumers

A Giant Sucking Sound

The Internet's ability to disrupt supply chains has been recounted in countless books and articles. But it is the Internet's synergy with globalization that has had the most profound effect on supply chains in manufacturing. This synergy is best expressed by a model I call the technology/globalization vortex.

We have all watched water swirl its way down a drain. And we know how the spiral on the top surface of the water spins relatively slowly, and then as the spiral works its way down and approaches the drain, the water spins increasingly faster. This succinctly explains the action of the technology/globalization vortex. Technology facilitates globalization, and global entities (companies, organizations, cultures, governments, etc.) then demand better technology, which leads to more efficient globalization, and so on. However, each subsequent technological leap forward comes more quickly than the last, speeding up the vortex effect. This phenomenon is neither a product of the modern age nor a product of the Internet. Rather, the vortex has been spinning for centuries, and the Internet is simply a link in the chain of technologies that compels the vortex to spin ever faster.

For example, the availability of information and how quickly we access it has evolved from handwritten documents viewed only by an elite few, to printed pages, to faxed messages, to e-mail. And with each technological leap forward, the information is delivered more quickly to an increasingly wider audience. It took thirty-eight years to build a fifty-million-person consumer base for radio and ten years to build a fifty-million-person consumer base for cable television. For the Internet? Five years. The sourcing and delivery of goods is another example. From caravans to trains to trucks, clipper ships to ocean freighters to cargo planes, each incremental improvement in technology has led to more and increasingly faster globalization.

How did the twin effects of technology and globalization affect supply chains? The Internet is an agent of disintermediation. What is disintermediation? It's a fancy way of saying that if your company is situated in the middle of a distribution network and you add cost to the process without adding enough value to justify the cost, you can kiss your company good-bye because it will not survive. Any distribution network with multiple links survives only because each link adds the requisite amount of value to justify its cost. When a link is no longer perceived to justify its added cost, it becomes disintermediated and dies. Think travel agencies and brick-and-mortar stores that sell recorded music. When people began buying travel and music directly over the Internet, the travel agencies and record stores no longer added the value that made them worth the increased markup.

The fastest growing smartphone company in China is Xiaomi. Xiaomi's business model is to copy the features of Apple and Samsung products and sell them at near cost directly to the consumer online, bypassing retailers altogether. The company's CEO, Lei Jun, claims that his mission is to "change the world's view of Chinese products."[51] He figures that he will accomplish that mission by selling a smartphone just as good as Apple's or Samsung at half the price. Then, he'll use the Gillette model (sell the razor cheap and generate profits from the sale of razor blades) and make most of his money selling apps for the phone. This will not change the world's view of Chinese products because Xiaomi is not truly changing the China manufacturing business model; as most Chinese manufacturers have done, he is simply reverse engineering another brand's product and then selling it at a lower price. His innovation is disintermediating smartphone retailers in order to sell the phone at the lower price.

Disintermediation doomed Quill and Just-A-Stretch. When the US textile business was healthy, the entire supply chain existed here. But then the combination of low wages in China, the ability to more quickly share information over the Internet, and the technology of more efficient overseas transportation logistics eventually sucked the apparel supply chain to China. A company like Just-A-Stretch that was one small piece of a textile supply chain could not continue to exist in the United States if the remainder of the supply chain was now in Asia. If goods had to move from China to Just-A-Stretch and then back to China, the value the company added would be out of line with the costs incurred by moving the goods back and forth across the Pacific Ocean.

As wages have risen in China, some elements of the apparel supply chain have migrated to Vietnam, Bangladesh, and other low-cost countries. But this migration will take time because, for greatest efficiency, *the entire supply chain* must migrate. The supply chain must also have access to transportation logistics such as roads, bridges, and ports so that products can be moved expeditiously. Thus, geographical proximity is now vital to the efficiency of supply chains. Isabelle Benoit's greatest challenge when establishing Bullet Blues as a US apparel manufacturer was trying to recreate an entire supply chain that had virtually disappeared from our shores.

Quill was disintermediated by the manner in which information readily available over the Internet allowed promotional products suppliers, distributors, and advertisers to directly source promotional products in China. Keep in mind that the promotional products distribution network was originally built on the principle of hiding information. Advertisers could neither identify nor locate manufacturers. The Internet changed that. The capability of buyers, distributors, and importers to source directly, combined with the low cost of writing instruments manufactured in China and more efficient shipping logistics, put pricing pressure on Quill. That pricing pressure led to stressed margins, lower sales, and Quill's eventual demise as a family-owned manufacturing business.

The technology/globalization vortex is no one's fault; it's simply a fact of life. The decisions of government, individual companies, and consumers can feed into that effect and speed it up, but we can't slow it down, and we can't stop it.

David vs. Goliath

A report released in 2013 by the MIT Taskforce on Innovation and Production noted that some of the fastest growing US companies of the past thirty years, including companies such as Dell, Cisco, Apple, and Qualcomm, have almost no domestic manufacturing capability. Why? The task force places the blame squarely on 1980s' financial markets that placed higher valuations on "asset-light" companies. The report notes that "first among the business functions that companies started moving out of their own corporate walls was manufacturing—for that produced reductions in headcount and capital costs that stock markets immediately rewarded."[52] Wall Street turned manufacturing into nothing more than a cost center. This purely financial strategy, while effective for improving the bottom line over the short term, led to the massive offshoring of manufacturing jobs, particularly after China's entry into the WTO. By throwing manufacturing employees out of work, money was taken from the pockets of US consumers that had traditionally been customers of those same companies.

How did that affect small, family-owned companies like Quill and Just-A-Stretch? Extremely low wages in countries like China led larger companies to offshore to reduce manufacturing costs. In order to remain competitive against low-wage overseas manufacturers, smaller domestic companies had to slash margins at the same time that their revenue was decreasing. Ultimately, the math no longer added up, and companies either closed (Just-A-Stretch) or were sold to companies that were already offshoring (Quill). Fruit of the Loom's decision to ditch Just-A-Stretch as a supply chain partner was based solely on a financial calculation. There was no transition to cushion the blow or an option for Laferriere, as a longtime supply chain partner, to sharpen his pencil and narrow the pricing gap.

So this is also an issue of large companies vs. small. Large companies, especially multinational brands, manufacturers, and large financial services companies are vocal proponents of trade agreements because many have come close to maximizing their market share in the United States. Each additional dollar of US sales revenue is tougher to get due to the level of competition here. For them, the biggest revenue upside is in emerging markets like China. So they favor trade deals that lower trade barriers *into* an emerging market, even if the deal is skewed in favor of manufacturers in the emerging market country and against domestic manufacturers. In their book *Producing Prosperity*, Willy Shih and Gary Pisano quote the American CEO of a US multinational company expressing reluctance about taking a pro-US business stance. He said, "As an American, I am rooting for the American economy, but half my management team are not Americans, and more than half my employees work outside the U.S. So for me to tell them as CEO that I want to do something good for America is not necessarily a message they are going to be all that excited about."[53]

Take a look at the roster of membership and the list of board members of the US-China Business Council (www.uschina.org), which lobbies to expand commercial relationships between the United States and China. You won't see many names of smaller companies like Quill or

Just-A-Stretch. Council membership is composed primarily of companies more interested in selling into China than rocking the boat with China over unfair trading practices. In a January 2013 report entitled "China and the U.S. Economy: Advancing a Winning Trade Agenda," the Council strongly defended more liberal trade policies with China. Some of their positions in this report included:

- Let's move on from China's currency manipulation to issues that really do matter.
- We have options when China doesn't play fair—like the WTO.
- Investment from China supports jobs in America.[54]

China currency manipulation is not an issue? Though he does nothing about it, even the US Treasury Secretary continues to insist that China manipulates its currency to the detriment of US manufacturers. And do you really believe that we should put faith in the WTO to pass judgment on our trade policy? Keep in mind that this is the same WTO that recently ruled the United States should not force meat producers to put a country of origin label on their products. Seems reasonable to me to want to know where the meat you are about to eat came from, but the WTO thinks otherwise. And as to investment from China supporting jobs in America? Sure it does, but keep in mind that some of those US companies are selling at a distressed price precisely because of offshoring and the resulting inability to compete against imports. Meanwhile, the Chinese direct foreign investment money used to fund those acquisitions comes largely from selling products—made with cheap labor in substandard working conditions—that they export to the United States

This is not to demonize the people who run large companies. They are, for the most part, playing by the rules and performing their responsibility to make their companies financially successful. Larger companies will, of course, lobby for trade deals when those deals are in their best interest. But it is an unfortunate fact that there are winners and losers in every trade agreement. Unfortunately, domestic manufacturers—especially small to medium-size US manufacturers—have been thrown under the bus by past and present administrations when negotiating trade deals to the benefit of multinationals and large financial services firms.

Another mistake that individual companies of all sizes have made is neglecting to determine whether offshoring truly reduces their costs, especially now that prices on many imports are rising. Instead of merely comparing the price of a part or product made domestically vs. overseas, they should take a closer look at what is called the total cost of ownership. The total cost of ownership includes variables above and beyond the price of the product itself. Those variables include transportation costs, minimum order sizes, supply chain risk (port disruptions, political instability, etc.), and a number of other factors that are often ignored when comparing the price of an imported and a domestically made item. In a March 2015 report to Congress, the Commerce Department encouraged companies that are now offshoring to use a total cost of ownership approach when comparing the cost of US-made product to those made by an overseas source. This approach not only lowers costs but also spurs innovation.[55] Companies would be wise to keep in mind that the price of an item is not necessarily the total cost.

Then there is the failure of individual smaller companies to adapt to the new global environment. In my relatively brief experience in the textile business, one of the biggest challenges I have encountered is the service level of the domestic webbing vendors whose companies have been devastated by the migration of apparel manufacturing to China. Many are now surviving, for the most part, on business that is either highly regulated (e.g., seat belt strapping for the automotive industry) or the result of US government set-aside programs. Several of the domestic houses with which I've dealt seem not to have learned the lessons of the webbing migration to China.

I have often needed samples of new webbing and/or short production runs to test new products. Procuring from a US vendor a sample of a new webbing style or width to show a customer is usually an agonizingly slow process. China webbing manufacturers generally respond much more quickly to sample requests than US companies. It seems that the reliance on longer-run set-aside business has actually enabled the US-based webbing manufacturers to continue their bad habits from days long past.

Being relatively new to the textile industry, it has amazed me that so many of the few remaining survivors of the domestic webbing business have missed the lessons of the last fifty years. For the most part, they seem to be keeping their eyes on the brass ring of large orders from regulated industries, propping up their obsolete business model, and turning their backs on small projects with big potential because they view them as too much trouble to pursue. Meanwhile, as with Just-A-Stretch, the loss of one important customer could put them out of business.

"You're Entitled to Your Own Opinion, But Not Your Own Facts"[56]

In December 2014, in a push to be granted trade promotion authority, President Obama stated, "While there's no doubt that some manufacturing moved offshore in the wake of China entering the WTO and as a consequence of NAFTA, more of those jobs were lost because of automation and capital investment." He went on to say, "Over time, growth, investment, exports all have increased the capacity for working families to improve their economic standing."[57] It is precisely these types of unquestioned presumptions by past and present administrations that have landed us in this predicament.

The president was incorrect when he said that trade agreements have given working families an increased capacity to improve their economic standing. In reality, median household income in the United States, adjusted for inflation, has *dropped* since China's 2002 entry into the WTO. Thus, freer trade has not meant greater prosperity for US families. It's time to revisit the old economic saw that any type of trade deal that brings in lower-priced imports somehow magically raises the standard of living in the United States The statistics clearly show that's not the case. It is precisely this type of faulty logic that has led to misguided trade policies such as Clinton's push for China to enter the WTO and Obama's push for the Trans-Pacific Partnership trade agreement.

There is nothing wrong with reciprocal trade agreements or trade policies with trading partners who work to keep the playing field level. But that has clearly not been the case, and our ability to pay less for a T-shirt from Bangladesh or a pair of shoes from China has not raised the standard of living in the United States. Why? It's simple common sense. Even though we may be importing goods that are cheaper than if they were manufactured here, we're putting people out of work to do it. And if we're putting people out of work, the standard of living won't go up. One needn't be an economist to figure that out.

The idea that automation is more responsible than offshoring for the loss of manufacturing jobs is also highly debatable. A comprehensive March 2012 report released by the Information and Innovation Technology Foundation, *Worse Than the Great Depression: What Experts Are Missing about Manufacturing Decline*, compared the ratio of productivity increases to manufacturing job loss in the 1990s and the 2000s. Their exhaustive analysis determined that the massive loss of US manufacturing jobs since China's entry into the WTO was not caused by increases in productivity. Indeed, the report states that "the ratio of manufacturing productivity to overall business productivity was approximately the same in both decades. Yet in the 1990s manufacturing jobs were essentially unchanged." The report notes that during the 1990s, manufacturing jobs fell by 1 percent, while productivity increased 53 percent. In the following decade, after China's entry into the WTO, productivity increased 66 percent, and manufacturing jobs fell 33 percent. It is highly unlikely that a 13 percent difference in the percentage increase in productivity caused the percentage of manufacturing job loss to increase from 1 percent to 33 percent.[58] Clearly automation was not the primary cause of the historic loss of manufacturing jobs in the last decade.

US trade policy has, in general, been predicated on the wrong assumptions. Of course, in the end, that policy is more greatly influenced by the roster of companies in the US-China Business Council than it is by the thousands of small to midsize companies that have been either eliminated or decimated by offshoring. As previously noted, large multinational companies are far more interested in selling into China than in protecting small to midsize US manufacturers against unfair trade practices, and it's the multinationals that have the ear of Washington, DC. Goliath has deeper pockets than David.

I Have Met the Enemy, and the Enemy …

Mere weeks before its scheduled product launch, Apple made a big design change to the glass screens on its iPhone. The first shipment of the new glass screens was delivered to the floor of the Chinese factory at midnight. At the plant, the foreman immediately awakened eight thousand workers inside the company's dormitories. They hastily threw on their clothes, headed across the road to the factory, lined up for a biscuit and a cup of tea, and began the assembly process of ten thousand iPhones per day with the redesigned part. It was 1:00 a.m.[59]

How did it come to pass that one of the most successful companies of the last fifty years—whose phenomenal growth was fueled by the US consumer—ends up doing its manufacturing at Foxconn in China?

For the complete answer, we cannot point the finger only at government trade policies and large multinational companies. We must also take a long, hard look in the mirror. For we are all responsible to some degree when we refuse to pay a premium—no matter how small— for products made in the United States. When a US B2B buyer or a consumer is unwilling to pay that premium, it forces US manufacturers to make cheaper, lower-quality products to compete with the lower-priced imports. Of course, this only feeds the offshoring monster because as the quality of the US-made product declines, it drives more buyers away.

Sometimes, it's not even a question of paying more, but of taking the time to look at the label and determine the country of origin before we buy. I'm as guilty as anyone. In the interest of expediency or a better price, we just buy what we've always bought or, if it's a product new to us, neglect to check where it's made before we buy.

It is more expedient for us to blame companies, politicians, or macroeconomic forces beyond our control. After all, so we rationalize, the business manager is faced with the simple choice of keeping production stateside or taking it overseas. The patriotic thing to do is keep it here. However, when the leaders of a company are faced with the stark decision of choosing either the survival of their business or loyalty to US manufacturing, almost all will choose the survival of the business. And if that business leader makes a decision to keep manufacturing stateside based on the belief that the B2B buyer or consumer will take the time and effort to ensure that the product they purchase is made in the United States of America *and* that the buyer or consumer will pay a premium for that product, that business leader will be whistling past the graveyard, as I once did. I was naïve enough to believe that nationalism trumped the pocketbook, and it lulled me to sleep as China manufacturers slowly but inexorably took market share from Quill. Relying on the patriotism of the general consumer is not a business model; it's not even a reasonable marketing strategy.

So we must cast a broad net when attempting to round up the culprits of the offshoring boom. Fortunately, the marketplace is now slowly changing in ways that are negatively affecting low-cost overseas producers, particularly China, and opening a window of opportunity for smart, nimble US manufacturers competing with overseas companies. I saw that window open—and discovered how to slip through it—when a small US manufacturer presented me with a second chance to battle the imports.

Back to the Future

As the Woonasquatucket River meanders toward downtown Providence, it runs a gauntlet of hulking red brick sentinels—grand old factory buildings that once housed thriving manufacturers. Some are now in a state of transition to mixed-use development projects—commercial, residential, and retail. Others remain vacant or near vacant.

One bright, cold morning in February 2006, I dodged the potholes as I pulled into a deteriorating parking lot adjacent to one of those old brick sentinels, the site of what is now called the American Locomotive Works (ALCO). The original factory on the site, built for the Rhode Island Locomotive Works in the late 1800s, was subsequently bought by ALCO, who added additional buildings. In 1898 the United States Rubber Company bought the property. After they abandoned Providence, the site became the home of jewelry manufacturers, platers, assembly operations, and textile companies. As those industries gradually moved to China, the factory floor space was partitioned and leased to downsizing manufacturers trying to hang on, companies in need of warehouse storage, artists using tax credits to lease loft space, and a myriad of small start-up enterprises. I walked through a battered metal door marked 25 Eagle St. and climbed a set of well-worn steps to a door marked Trans-Tex LLC to meet with Phil Barr and Adrien "Skip" Hebert.

Barr and Hebert began their careers as a lawyer and a CPA, respectively. In those roles they were involved in the expansion—and eventual sale—of a safety products company based in Smithfield, Rhode Island. After the successful completion of that deal, they banded together in hopes of acquiring a small local company with upside potential. That search led them to a small dye sublimation printer in Providence, Trans-Tex, which they acquired in 2004.

Dye sublimation printing is a two-step process that permanently decorates long, narrow strips of polyester webbing with multicolor designs. The first step is to print a pattern or logo with dye sublimation ink on a special paper. The narrow polyester fabric strips are then lined up with the pattern on the paper and run through a heat transfer machine. When the heat from the transfer machine comes in contact with the dye sublimation ink on the paper, the ink on the paper is transferred onto the fabric strips. Because it is a dyeing process, the resulting printed image is far more permanent than a screen-printed image that you might see, for example, on a souvenir T-shirt.

Although the primary market for dye sublimation printing had traditionally been the apparel market, Barr and Hebert noticed, during the due diligence period of the Trans-Tex acquisition, that the growth area for the company over the prior two years had been the sale of lanyards. If you have attended a trade show, you were probably given a lanyard before you entered the exhibit area. It is worn around the neck and typically holds a name badge, pen, tube of lip balm, or other small product. At most events, lanyards are printed with the event organizer's name or the logo of one of the event's sponsors.

Traditionally, lanyards are screen printed, which is a relatively slow, inexpensive process, more suited for shorter production runs and the reproduction of relatively uncomplicated logos in one or two colors. If an advertiser needs a large number of printed lanyards (2,500 units and up) or wants a complex multicolor design, dye sublimation printing is a more efficient and higher-quality process than screen printing. This provided an opportunity for both domestic and overseas dye sublimation printers.

Those US companies that had seen their business printing trim for apparel or furniture move increasingly overseas were looking for other products to print. Of course, at the same time, the dye sublimation printers in China who had hijacked the apparel business were aggressively pursuing the dye sublimated lanyard business here in the United States. With the proliferation of trade shows and event marketing and the subsequent increase in the marketing and distribution of lanyards, this small niche market of dye sublimated lanyards was attractive both to the handful of narrow web dye sublimation printers who still survived in the United States and to China printers.

Why would US promotional products suppliers outsource dye sublimated lanyards to China instead of simply producing them themselves? Because the barrier to entry for dye sublimation printing is relatively high. Unlike the low start-up costs for producing screen-printed lanyards, long-run dye sublimation flexography presses are expensive and require a particular level of expertise. Since the dye sublimated segment of the lanyard market has traditionally been a relatively small percentage of the total lanyard market, US lanyard suppliers outsourced the manufacturing of dye sublimated lanyards rather than incur the high start-up costs to enter the dye sublimation printing business.

Barr and Hebert sensed that the lanyard business had a strong upside, but they had no direct experience navigating the complexities of the promotional products distribution network. They knew that the lion's share of lanyards were sold through the promotional products distribution channel and hoped to identify someone who already knew the business and had relationships with some of the key suppliers and distributors. When we met at a promotional products trade show in Las Vegas, they invited me over to Trans-Tex after we returned home to discuss how I might help them.

Because the company had traditionally survived on the long production runs of the apparel and strap business, the number of orders in-house on any given day was relatively small. On my first visit to Trans-Tex, I was struck by how the orders were parceled out one-by-one at the beginning of each day. Few true production management systems were in place, and orders were entered into the rudimentary software system after the order was shipped. Before it was invoiced, the only record of the order was the job bag that passed from department to department. On occasion, job bags had been lost on the factory floor, and orders simply disappeared until the customer called to inquire when they would be shipped.

Personnel were more attuned to the relatively slow production pace of a manufacturing operation, with fewer orders and longer runs. Much of the time was spent monitoring the current job that was running. Even so, print quality was generally unpredictable. The sales and customer service staffs were helpful but generally inexperienced and ill-suited temperamentally to handling the stress and strains if the company were to grow quickly. One might best describe the operation at that time as slow on its feet.

As a one-day-per-week consultant, I spent the first few months learning about dye sublimation printing, becoming acquainted with the business model of key customers, and implementing some rudimentary process changes in customer service and production. And although those changes improved operations, more radical changes would be necessary if Trans-Tex was to position itself for dramatic growth.

The most glaring need was for someone to run the business day-to-day. The three of us agreed that the long-term upside of the company was in the lanyard business, but the company needed someone to manage it who knew the ins and outs of the promotional products business, understood the distribution network, had a personal relationship with the key players, and could have a short-term impact on sales while putting the pieces in place for future growth. Both Barr and Hebert were involved in monitoring day-to-day operations, but neither wanted to assume a managerial role.

Finally, after a cursory search for prospective candidates, Barr and Hebert asked if I would be willing to act as their CEO, if only on a part-time basis. My initial reaction was negative. International Marketing Advantages, my own business, was doing well, and spending the majority of my time at Trans-Tex would prevent me from building my own company. In addition, Trans-Tex was clearly a slow-footed company tethered to a fading apparel industry.

But before I delivered a polite refusal to Barr and Hebert, two memories from past career positions came to mind. Around 1980, while still in the retail sportswear business, I heard a salesman for one of the apparel brands tell a story about visiting a factory in China that made blue jeans for his company. As he walked the factory floor, he saw thousands of jeans being sewn, but also noticed that the crew was working on three different brands, including his, in the same factory. The other memory was from the days when Quill was exploring the possibility of overseas manufacturing. Our product development manager returned from a trip to a writing instrument factory in China and saw, on the same factory floor, pens being assembled for several different writing instrument brands.

These recollections led me to an epiphany. Could Trans-Tex implement a strategy here in the United States similar to that of a China manufacturer? Could we turn the distribution strategy of China manufacturers against them? Since lanyards are essentially a commodity product that is customized in the printing and assembly process, could Trans-Tex be successful selling lanyards to multiple US promotional products supplier companies and then depend on those supplier companies to market them to distributors and advertisers?

Personal experience led me to believe the answer was no. Not that those supplier companies were not great marketers. But for several years I had argued that distribution networks were flattening and that technology-driven disintermediation would put any company at risk that was in the middle of a lengthy distribution channel. I had witnessed it in the writing instrument business and the apparel business. And if a US manufacturer could not win that battle with pens or blue jeans (or cars or toys or computers), how could Trans-Tex win that battle producing low-cost lanyards?

It seemed that the only chance at success in implementing this strategy rested on three clear principles. Trans-Tex had to assemble and ship smaller quantities than China sources were willing to produce. For smaller quantity orders, the shipping costs from Asia would partly negate the advantage of lower labor rates at China factories.

Secondly, due to the event-driven nature of the promotional products business, Trans-Tex would need to ship product faster, sometimes within hours. Advertisers were making buying decisions closer to the moment of need, and if Trans-Tex could always fill that immediate need, China manufacturers could not match that speed to market.

Finally, I knew that what most worried US advertisers and distributors about bypassing US supplier companies and sourcing product directly overseas was the risk factor. Should something go wrong with the order, either product or imprint quality, there was no recourse. And even if there was, the event would be long over before a replacement order could be shipped from China. So Trans-Tex would need to always produce better quality than our overseas competitors.

Ultimately the strategy depended on these three bedrock principles—*fewer, faster,* and *finer.* Trans-Tex had to develop the capability of producing smaller quantities faster and with higher product quality than China competitors. Any one or two of these was not sufficient. In this head-to-head confrontation with China manufacturers, Trans-Tex would need to consistently do all three extremely well, every day, with every order, to even survive.

Then there was the "trust" factor. Competing US promotional products suppliers might buy from the same factory in China because they presumed that the China source would not be able to compete with them on their own turf. But would several domestic supplier competitors order from the same US factory given that the US factory could more easily gain access to their customers than a Pacific Rim manufacturer? It was clear to me that domestic suppliers would do so only if they could trust the US manufacturer to support the promotional products distribution channel, refuse to market or sell to their customers, and keep their relationship confidential from competing suppliers.

These were the factors I weighed while considering the offer from Barr and Hebert. Taking the CEO slot at Trans-Tex, even though part-time, was certainly a gamble. Successful or not, if I spent a considerable number of hours there, I incurred the opportunity cost of not developing my own consulting business. I would essentially be relegating my own fledgling company to a fraction of my time. Given the prospective business model I was considering for Trans-Tex, the chances for success were uncertain. The company seemed to be sputtering along, stuck in a difficult strategic position with precious few escape options. Also, after my time at Quill building what was largely a start-up manufacturing operation, the Trans-Tex position seemed, in many ways, a step backward into a world I had left long ago.

F. Scott Fitzgerald once famously wrote that there are no second acts in American lives. But whether it was the comfort level I felt in a small-business environment, the rapport I had developed with Barr and Hebert, a weakness to champion a long shot, or the urge to test a new, untried business model, I decided to take the position as part-time CEO of Trans-Tex and put Fitzgerald's maxim to the test.

Several weeks after I took on this new role, the real estate developer Streuver Bros. Eccles & Rouse bought the old brick sentinel on the Woonasquatucket River that housed Trans-Tex, forcing us to move to a new location. Our landlord, Licht Properties, happened to have space available in a mostly empty building nearby, one-half block from my first office with the kitchen sink and ironing board in the old tenement at the former Quill site. After looking at two or three other options in Providence, we settled on the facility offered by Licht, the "Flair Building," so named because the front of the building still held the name of a longtime former tenant. Flair had been a manufacturer of Plexiglas point-of-purchase displays for local jewelers and pen manufacturers. In my position at Quill, I had been one of their customers before the retail display industry largely closed up shop in the United States and moved to China.

This seemed an echo of an ominous past for US companies like Trans-Tex. But the die was cast; I was staking the future of Trans-Tex on an untested business model of competing directly with the juggernaut of low-cost China manufacturing companies. Would this new location for Trans-Tex, the former site of an offshoring victim, continue to be haunted by the mistakes of the past, or could we transform it into ground zero for a renaissance by implementing the principles of *fewer, faster,* and *finer*? Millions of dollars and the jobs of new friends and old would hang in the balance.

CHAPTER 4

The Making of Less—Producing *Fewer*

Appear where they cannot go...[60]
The Art of War

The Foxconn factory in Longhua, Shenzen, is not a typical factory. It's more reminiscent of a company town created at the beginning of the US industrial revolution—only far larger. The sprawling complex, covering over one square mile, contains its own television station, fire brigade, and hospital. Hundreds of thousands of people work there. In many ways, it is the epitome of the overseas low-cost manufacturing business model, created to produce literally millions of the exact same thing over and over and over again. It is a manufacturing juggernaut designed almost exclusively to exploit the concept of economy of scale—and it is slowly becoming obsolete.

I've Got My Own

People increasingly want products and services that are tailored to their own individual preferences. When I first entered the manufacturing world back in the 1980s, I was struck by how many US factories focused on selling what they could make instead of first determining what the customer wanted and then finding a way to make it. And companies survived quite well doing that until, like Quill or Just-A-Stretch, their customers slowly disappeared, taken by companies that could do exactly the same thing but do it a lot cheaper. If there is one dominant characteristic of the US consumer since the beginning of the mass production-driven consumer era, it is the focus on finding the lowest-priced widget you can find. It doesn't matter where or how it was made; only that it is the cheapest. But the consumer, particularly the US consumer, is changing in radical ways. The concept of having exactly what one wants—as opposed to a "one size fits all" mentality—is becoming hardwired into today's consumers, particularly those in the United States.

People once walked into a diner and ordered a cup of coffee. You had basically two options, regular or decaffeinated. The server would give you the cup of coffee, and you would add your own cream and sugar. Then came Starbucks. Starbucks is a pioneer in what is now being called "mass customization," which is simply defined as making more personal choices available to a mass market of customers. After Starbucks, a plain cup of coffee was no longer good enough, and other coffee purveyors were forced to respond. What is Dunkin' Donuts today but a working-class version of Starbucks? Walk into almost any coffee shop, and the options are almost overwhelming. Regular coffee, espresso, cappuccinos, lattes, decaf, hot, or iced, all with a myriad of flavor options, plus cream, milk, skim milk, soy milk, almond milk, and so on.

For the first forty years of its history, Lay's sold two types of potato chips: regular and BBQ. In the late '70s, sour cream and onion was introduced, and since then the company has unleashed a flood of new flavors and styles. The company recently held an online poll that allowed their customers to choose whether their next new flavor would be ginger wasabi, mango salsa, or cheddar bacon mac and cheese. The winner will be added to options that now include dill pickle and pico de gallo. In fact, there are now fifty-four different combinations of chip styles and flavors listed on the Lay's website. What explains the fevered pace of new flavor introductions in the second half of its history? It's not that the individual consumer wants a wider assortment of flavors; it's that we are looking for our own particular flavor.

Some may recall putting on a record album and listening to songs you did not particularly care for because you had to hear every song on the album side in order to hear the ones you really liked—unless you wanted to go to the trouble of picking up the needle and moving it to the desired track. Now we create our own digital music playlists and listen only to the songs we love. And Google recently announced the launch of a music subscription service that anticipates your mood and plays what it thinks you will want to hear based on your past habits and the time of day and/or venue. So not only do you now have the option of listening only to the songs you love, but this service actually anticipates and plays those songs you may want to hear at a particular time of day based on how you are feeling.

Catering to individual preferences is even becoming a standard solution to perk up tired brands. What is McDonald's solution to its current financial doldrums? Shake up its predictable menu and attract younger customers by launching a new program dubbed "Create Your Taste." Rolled out to roughly one in seven locations in 2015, customers order burgers from touch screens, choose from a variety of options including type of bun, sauce, and toppings, and then sit down and have the order delivered to their table. It's an updated and expanded version of the Burger King "Have It Your Way" campaign that revolutionized fast food several decades ago. McDonald's is now also offering breakfast all day to cater to those with odd schedules and those (mostly younger people) who simply like breakfast at any time of day. With the launch of these two initiatives, the company's fortunes are rebounding. Why? Because they are catering to individual preferences.

I've long been frustrated by the way cable television companies force us to buy a bundle of channels rather than allowing us to pick and choose specific channels. If I want to watch old films on Turner Classic Movies (TCM), I shouldn't be forced to pay for twenty other channels to get TCM. However, it's only a matter of time before I (and millions of others) get what I want; the cable TV business model of selling bundled packages of channels is doomed to fail in this new consumer environment.

"The technology of Internet-delivered TV programming is swamping the argument of whether cable operators ought to bundle or unbundle the cable channels," says Patrick Parsons, a professor at Pennsylvania State University's College of Communications.[61] So, not only are consumers demanding they have exactly the channels they want, but the Internet is facilitating the process. Parsons likens the debate about whether cable channels will be unbundled to an argument "about whether there should be headlights on buggies."

In his book *The Long Tail*, Chris Anderson noted that throughout history, lockstep culture—that is, everybody wanting and having exactly the same thing—is the exception, not the rule. However, the industrial revolution and its resultant mass urbanization spawned mass media and mass culture. The Internet is tearing apart mass culture and driving the importance of the *fewer* principle. Anderson noted that "in an era without the constraints of physical shelf space and other bottlenecks of distribution, narrowly targeted goods and services can be as economically attractive as mainstream fare."[62]

Dell revolutionized the personal computer business in the '90s with a business model that allowed consumers to "customize" their laptops by choosing features and software programs within a menu of options. They then bypassed the retailer to ensure speed to market and the lowest price.

A recent article in *Industry Week* characterized this trend as "the consumerization of manufacturing." Driven by consumer demand for more customized products, "retailers struggling to keep up are putting pressure back on manufacturers to deliver more customized formulations, packages, and configurations for all kinds of products." Nike is cited as a brand at the forefront of allowing consumers to customize their products through their NIKEiD program.[63]

Why Less Is More

This sea change in consumer preferences toward more customized products exposes a key weakness in the manufacturing business model of juggernauts like Foxconn. Conceived and designed to produce commodity products at the lowest possible price, most Pacific Rim manufacturing operations are focused almost exclusively on long production runs. Given their distance from the United States and the costs for transportation, they must produce long runs in order to keep prices low. And they need to ship a lot of product at the same time in order to keep shipping costs low.

China manufacturers are slow to adapt to the demands of the new consumer. Liu Jun, vice president and chief creative officer of Eego

Cultural Industry Investment Company and once named one of the "50 Most Creative Individuals in China" by *New Ad Magazine*, characterizes this weakness as the lack of a global vision. He believes that Chinese companies, in general, do not have what he calls the "user-centeredness" that is central to Western design thought. He goes on to say that "Chinese designers only think about what pleasures them, not the customer."[64]

US manufacturers can exploit this weakness by implementing the *fewer* principle. The *fewer* principle holds that a manufacturing company should focus on shorter runs and/or more customized products. Product development efforts should tend *away* from low-cost commodity items and tend *toward* products that can be manufactured in shorter runs or that are customizable. Investment in plant and equipment should be considered in light of whether that investment makes the operation more flexible, better able to produce shorter runs and/or better able to customize a product. It goes against the grain of their business model for overseas manufacturers to revamp their factories for short production runs or to create customized products. And even if they did, those companies would still confront the cost inefficiency of shipping smaller quantities halfway around the world.

During the last decade, as imports from China decimated furniture manufacturing in North Carolina, those with the best chance of surviving changed their business model to allow retailers to order smaller quantities and to allow consumers to order more customized products. After China manufacturers began selling directly to retailers (bypassing the same US manufacturers that had become their importers), the Vaughan-Bassett furniture line began offering retail dealers occasional tables and consoles in much smaller quantities than a China manufacturer could. The products were preassembled and available in six colors. John Bassett III, chairman of the Vaughan-Bassett Company, noted that "the smaller guys (retailers) we cater to, they can't bring in containers of these (from China)"[65] (parentheses mine). Bassett Furniture responded to the China onslaught by releasing a line of casual dining furniture in their own stores that was custom assembled and finished, then delivered in ten days. The consumer could use an in-store computer to choose from forty-two colors and a thousand different fabrics. "We can make just one single piece if we want," said Bassett CEO Rob Spilman.[66]

If there is any industry that qualifies as the canary in the mine when it comes to reshoring, it is the apparel industry. In 1960, the United States manufactured 95 percent of the apparel that Americans purchased; today 97 percent is imported. Yet increasing costs out of China and the trend toward customization are leading some apparel manufacturing back to the United States. Boathouse Sports, based in Philadelphia, designs and manufactures performance apparel for teams across the globe. Their hallmark is the ability to customize their garments and deliver them quickly. Founder and owner John Strotbeck, who started the business in the 1980s, describes his company's niche as "mass customization of athletic wear, short runs and speed. We offer mass customization at its best."[67]

Also from the apparel world, have you ever been frustrated by the three standard options of shirt sizes (S, M, L), none of which fits you well? After his girlfriend made fun of his baggy button-down shirt, Matt Hornbuckle decided to do something about it. He partnered with a coworker and founded Stantt, a New Jersey-based manufacturer of men's shirts. They used a Kickstarter campaign to raise over $100,000 to start the company and now offer seventy-five shirt sizes to accommodate a broad range of different body types. They're not customized, but they're close—and they're made in the United States of America.

Davis Industries, a manufacturer of canvas bags, beats the imports by benchmarking their overseas competitor's minimum order size and then reducing their own to 10 percent of those competitors, far below traditional industry standards. How? By making a modest investment in new production technology that allowed them to manufacture smaller quantities with lower setup costs. They also moved smaller orders into what was formerly their "fast-track" sample production line so these orders would not be stuck in the queue behind larger orders that took more time. Finally, they lowered setup charges to remove a significant hurdle to new orders, calculating that they would recoup those costs in repeat orders. Their CFO fretted about the operational costs of those smaller orders, but I urged him to consider them marketing costs for customer acquisition and retention, not production expenses. Since implementing the change, their order count has quadrupled, and 90 percent of their orders use the new technology. Has the new technology displaced workers? Just the opposite—their workforce has almost doubled in size.

The secret to the success of Liberty Bottleworks, a Portland-based manufacturer of aluminum drinking bottles, is the customization factor. Liberty allows their online customers to choose the shape, size, color, and graphics for their bottle. "We stopped counting custom designs after about 20,000," said COO Ryan Clark in an *Industry Week* interview.[68] "Instead of having to make 10,000 bottles to make a profit, now I can do 100." Liberty uses lean manufacturing, just-in-time inventory, and digital technologies to enable their ability to make *fewer*.

3-D Is a Charm

Amara's Law states that we tend to overestimate the effect of a technology in the short run and underestimate the effect in the long run. So it was with the birth of the Internet, and so it will be with the proliferation of 3-D printing, the most extreme manifestation of the *fewer* principle in action. 3-D printers allow the user to manufacture one custom piece. They have actually been in use in industrial environments for decades, primarily for creating prototypes. However, over the last five years, prices for the machines have plummeted, and desktop versions have become widely available. This has spurred legions of makers to experiment with the technology, leading to further refinements in the technology and potential uses for the machines. Worldwide shipments of 3-D printers reached 217,350 units in 2015, up from 108,151 in 2014, according to Gartner, Inc., an information technology and research and advisory company. They also estimate that 3-D printer unit sales will more than double every year between 2015 and 2018, by which time worldwide shipments are forecast to reach more than 2.3 million.[69]

Although they have traditionally been used by large manufacturers to speed up the product development process, 3-D printers are nearer to making the leap to consumer products than many think. Nike has used 3-D printing to create custom sports bags, and in a recent interview, Under Armour's senior innovation design manager, when asked whether the company had any plans for 3-D printing, responded, "If you want to put something in your hat (figuratively), definitely something big is going to happen in the future." It sounds as though a cap tailored exactly to the shape of your head is in the works.[70]

In a January 2015 article on the availability of 3-D-printed shoes, Andrew Wheeler writes that "as the air of customization reaches the minds of an infinite number of consumers, the shoe shopping impetus is shifting from 'let's see what's available' to 'I want it to look exactly like this' or 'this is exactly what the shoe company should do' or 'why don't they just make them like this' and so on." Given the rapid proliferation of 3-D printers—and products made by them—one could substitute almost any word for "shoe."[71]

Local Motors, based in Phoenix, describes itself as a "free online and physical workspace where creativity, collaboration and design drive vehicle innovations." This online community, augmented by a small number of employees, designs, builds, and sells what they call "badass vehicles." Revenue is shared by those in the online community who helped create the product. At the January 2015 North American Auto Show in Detroit, Local Motors introduced a 3-D-printed car that can be made in forty hours. CEO Jay Rogers noted that fully 95 percent of the volume of the car is 3-D printed; the motor, springs, and tires are not.[72] It is apparent that Local Motors will eventually be offering car buyers the option of customizing body design, number and type of seats, trunk size, and so on. It will be some time before such vehicles are deemed safe for normal road conditions, but time is the only obstacle.

Even larger companies are exploring innovative ways to use 3-D printing. Let's say it's your anniversary, you are taking your spouse out for dinner, and you want the chef to serve pasta in the shape of a rose. You simply bring the rose design on a USB drive and hand it to your waiter, who passes it along to the chef. She installs the drive onto a 3-D printer and serves up the dish in twenty minutes. Seem far-fetched? The global pasta company Barilla is currently working with a research organization to design a 3-D pasta printer that will churn out custom-designed pasta at restaurant speed.[73] Also in the food realm, at the 2014 SXSW trade show in Austin, the Oreo booth featured two custom-made vending machines with a 3-D printer that enabled attendees to create and eat custom 3-D-printed Oreo cookies based on trending social conversations. Users picked from twelve "trending" flavors and colors of cream filling and then watched their cookie being "printed" in two minutes.[74]

Joshua Harris is working on a clothing printer that would allow you to create your own T-shirt at home, styled to your exact body type. When the garment begins to get a little ragged, you simply load it back into the printer, and it breaks down the thread for use in a new shirt.[75] The fact that 3-D printers will one day allow you to make your own clothing at home reminded me of an increasingly common sentiment I saw in the comments section at the end of an article concerning 3-D-printed dresses. Someone mentioned that it could be a lucrative revenue stream for the company selling the customized dresses, and one wag responded, "Sell it? Why? We can just easily replicate the pattern and print it ourselves. For the price (charged by the design company) you could buy a high end printer and do it yourself"[76] (parentheses mine).

Chris Anderson in *The Long Tail* was writing at the time about self-publishing, but his comments are just as applicable to 3-D printing. He writes, "Because the tools of production have entirely democratized, the population of producers is expanding exponentially, and now there's little stopping those with will and skill to create from doing just that."[77] 3-D printers have a synergistic relationship with the burgeoning consumer desire for more customized products, and they reinforce the importance of implementing the *fewer* principle in your manufacturing operation. They are here to stay, will become more affordable, and will increasingly be used not merely for prototypes, but for production runs. It may not be next year, but it will be within ten years.

Parts Are Products, Too

If you are a B2B manufacturer, you may be asking yourself, "How do these changing consumer habits affect my business? I don't manufacture consumer goods; I make an industrial part that is used in my customers' finished products." Keep in mind that the same people who have developed a craving for a niche flavor of potato chips and a half caffeinated vanilla latte with no foam are also working as purchasing managers at companies that buy parts. So they, too, will want precisely what they want, exactly when they want it. When you go to work, you don't check your personal preferences at the door.

B2B buyers are also under constant pressure to maintain lower parts inventories in order to improve their cash cycle and their companies' bottom lines. I saw this firsthand when visiting Vibco, a manufacturer of industrial vibrators based in Wyoming, Rhode Island. Vibco's founder and president, Karl Wadensten, is a noted proponent of lean manufacturing and just-in-time inventory positions. While touring the Vibco plant, I learned how they began sourcing certain parts and packaging locally in order to reduce both the cost of carrying inventory and the amount of space required to store that inventory. This can only be accomplished by geographically shortening the supply chain. Based on their lean business model, there are a number of parts at Vibco that can only be supplied by domestic manufacturers, particularly those in relatively close geographical proximity. An overseas manufacturer, with a business model built on making and shipping high quantities of a commodity-type product, is not in a position to fulfill certain sourcing needs for a company like Vibco.

As the price of goods from the Pacific Rim continues to rise, purchasing managers are beginning to realize that the price of a widget is not the same thing as the total cost of a widget. There are a number of factors in addition to the price that add to the cost of purchasing any good, but even more so for imports. One of those factors is the additional cost of buying large quantities. Most overseas manufacturers, in order to keep costs low, set high minimum order requirements. These high minimum order requirements force an importing company to lay out higher amounts of cash to get the best price. The opportunity cost of spending that cash, among other factors, must be added to the total cost of the product to arrive at its true price. By allowing the customer to buy *fewer*, a US manufacturer can keep those hidden costs lower.

Trans-Tex and the *Fewer* Principle

Why is the *fewer* principle so important to our success at Trans-Tex? Because for Trans-Tex, product customization is a given. Every order for lanyards, headbands, or wristbands is printed with a corporate logo and/

or slogan. When I first became involved with the company, the minimum order size for lanyards was one thousand pieces. The high minimum order size was due to the fact that Trans-Tex owned only high-speed flexography presses that were ideal for larger orders, but the long setup and teardown times and the cost of plates rendered those presses too costly for shorter runs. Knowing that the average order size in the promotional products business was continually shrinking, it was apparent that we needed to find a way to make smaller quantities. We also knew that it would be difficult for our competition in China to cost-effectively service small order requests for lanyards due to the much higher cost per piece of shipping smaller orders halfway around the world.

Producing shorter runs of lanyards had an immediate and notable impact on the number of orders flowing through the factory. After making the commitment and investment to manufacture shorter runs, order counts suddenly jumped. Between 2008 and 2009, the total order count increased 33 percent. Between 2009 and 2010, the increase was 61 percent. During 2014, Trans-Tex processed over 4.5 times the number of orders that were produced in 2007.

Such a dramatic increase in order count adds stress to any manufacturing process. And keep in mind that Trans-Tex was a small company without the resources to invest in top-of-the-line automation or processes. How did Trans-Tex cope? There were several key factors.

The first was the quality of its employees. In a small factory environment, it takes a special team to smoothly transition from an environment with a small number of large orders to one with a large number of small orders. Battle-tested people with a sense of urgency, resiliency, and the willingness to take ownership are essential to implementing the *fewer* principle.

Another key element is technology. The two key technology factors that enabled Trans-Tex to produce a larger number of small orders were the refinement of digital dye sublimation printing and the ability to directly download orders for custom products. We knew from the outset that our traditional flexography presses were the major hurdle. They were lightning-fast while running, but setup and teardown times were, by necessity, agonizingly slow. Thus, they were suitable only for longer runs. So we researched and invested in digital printers that were seventy-five times slower than the high-speed flexography presses. Seem counterintuitive to buy slower printing presses? Well, although they were much slower, they also required no setup or teardown time and no plates, and the printed paper they produced had relatively little effect on the balance of the manufacturing process. Thus, they were much more cost-effective for shorter runs and allowed Trans-Tex to drop the minimum order size to one hundred units.

The other important technology enhancement was the ability to download orders from large customers directly into our order entry system. Although this capability is de rigueur for many larger companies, particularly those dealing with big-box retailers, for a company the size of Trans-Tex it can be a stretch. However, Trans-Tex was buoyed by its own business model. Instead of bypassing supplier companies and selling to a high number of smaller distributor customers, we had chosen early on to sell to a handful of large supplier companies that were aggregating distributor orders. This meant that Trans-Tex was receiving a high volume of orders from only a few key customers, and computer programs could be more easily written to download a high percentage of the total orders received. If the business model were focused on servicing a large number of smaller customers, the company would have been faced with the prospect of hiring many more order entry and customer service people at the same time that they were investing in the plant and equipment to enable the production of a high number of smaller orders.

The third key element was reporting, that is, the ability to access data on what orders are in-house and where and what orders are scheduled to ship today. This seems simple, but keep in mind that Trans-Tex was producing a high number of customized orders, most of which were being shipped within twenty-four to seventy-two hours and traveling through five departments (order entry, art, printing, transfer, assembly). This is, of course, not unusual for an operation that simply pulls product off a shelf and ships it. But Trans-Tex was creating a lanyard product that was custom printed *and* sported several hundreds of options for attachments that needed to be hand-assembled to the printed narrow webbing. Obviously, keeping track of those in-house orders was essential. How did they do it? They had only a basic QuickBooks program that was built more for a distribution company than a manufacturer.

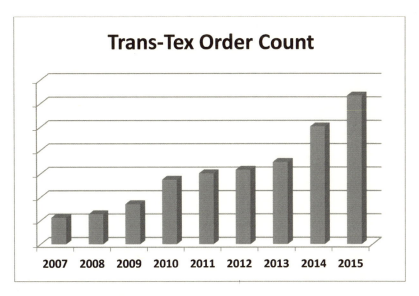

The left axis is purposely blank. Because it is a privately-held company, actual Trans-Tex order count is confidential information.

First, they were able to cull rudimentary in-house order data from the system, as most manufacturers can. Secondly, they invested in online portals that were connected to their biggest customers' IT systems, which allowed them to see the number and size of orders that would be coming within the next day or two. Thirdly, they installed a bar-coding system to internally track orders. Fourth, and most importantly, the people involved communicated—often. There were remarkably few formal meetings, but there were a slew of very brief one-on-one or two-on-one meetings throughout the course of a day between people in the company's five functional areas. Why not just a daily meeting? Because the landscape could change—and did change several times each day as new orders arrived requiring twenty-four- to seventy-two-hour turns. What was scheduled to ship today changed from hour to hour, if not minute by minute. Given the circumstances, it's not difficult to understand why the quality of the people at Trans-Tex was such a key to its success.

And, finally, another element that allowed Trans-Tex to cope with the proliferation of smaller orders was the ability to keep the order pipeline full. Turning around customized orders that pass through five departments in twenty-four hours means multiple shifts. Multiple shifts can only be cost-effective if there is consistently enough work to keep each shift sufficiently busy. It was, ultimately, the stellar performance of Trans-Tex that kept the pipeline full. The quick turn times of twenty-four to seventy-two hours (see next chapter) made it difficult for customers to insource production or find an alternate vendor. Phil Barr, one of Trans-Tex's owners, dubbed our company—to borrow a marketing slogan from Staples—the "easy button." By becoming experts at shipping small orders quickly, Trans-Tex simply made it difficult for customers to consider other options, so the flow continued through the production pipeline.

The capability of producing shorter runs of lanyards had ancillary benefits. Trans-Tex was also servicing the custom-printed ribbon market. Imagine going online or to a craft store around Valentine's Day and finding ribbon printed with hearts or flowers. Unlike the China ribbon manufacturers, which required long production runs of custom-printed product, we would service smaller online companies in quantities as low as one thousand yards. So, in the fall, for example, a ribbon distributor could order small production runs of ribbon printed with black cats or jack-o'-lanterns and resell them through their website in quantities as low as three yards to small crafts dealers and crafts enthusiasts all over the country.

The printed-ribbon business is driven largely by fresh patterns. When a distributor adds new patterns to their website, there is an immediate spike in business. Of course, if a ribbon distributor is constantly churning out new patterns on a seasonal basis, it is important to keep inventory levels of each pattern as low as possible. The Trans-Tex business model, built around short, customized production runs, made us the ideal supplier for that market.

The manufacturing business model of overseas low-cost manufacturers is focused almost exclusively on the long production run. This bias means that if you find yourself competing with those companies, implementing the *fewer* principle will be essential to winning the battle. That tendency on the part of our Pacific Rim competitors also leads them to sometimes miss out on great opportunities like Jerry the Bear. If you are an entrepreneur or a start-up company creating a niche product, Jerry's story illustrates why you should begin your supply chain search at home.

Not Your Average Bear

Adam pressed his face against the window as the car carrying his new friend pulled up to the curb outside his house. At five-and-a-half-years old, you feel more comfortable with a friend who shares your experiences, and none of Adam's young friends could understand what it was like to have diabetes. He had been told that Jerry the Bear could understand, so Adam was anxious to meet him.

Two strangers came out of the car, one of them carrying a plush bear that looked about twelve inches tall, held a glucometer in one hand, and sported a red backpack that made him look as though he was coming home from school. Adam guessed it must be Jerry. Adam's parents asked him to wait patiently while they opened the door and ushered in Jerry and the two young strangers who had designed and built him. What Adam didn't know was that the two young strangers were more nervous than he was.

Hannah Chung and Aaron Horowitz were those two young strangers. They met at Northwestern University while working on a Design for America project—a nationwide nonprofit focused on applying the concepts of "design thinking" to address high social-impact issues. "Design thinking" is a problem-solving protocol that involves intensively interviewing a target audience to develop new product ideas that solve a particular challenge. The group was given the challenge of designing a product to improve the lives of people living with type 1 diabetes.

While interviewing and observing doctors, parents, and children, they discovered that youngsters with type 1 diabetes habitually "injected" insulin into their plush toys and talked to them about their condition. Based on that feedback, Hannah and Aaron's team decided to create a plush bear with diabetic symptoms that children could monitor for glucose levels and treat when necessary. By learning to monitor the bear's condition, the child would better understand how to monitor and treat his or her own illness. Their idea won the prize as "Most Creative Submission" in Design for America's 2009 design challenge.

After putting together their first Jerry prototype, they knew they needed some real-world feedback from a child dealing with type 1 diabetes. Adam was the first young person to actually play with Jerry. After observing Adam's interaction with the bear and hearing his very direct feedback,

Aaron and Hannah went back to the drawing board to fine-tune the design. Each new iteration of Jerry went back to families for testing and feedback. After three years and twenty-nine prototypes, they had a design that was ready to go to market.

Jerry now had a monitor screen in his chest and insulin "injection points" on his thighs, backside, and the backs of his arms. A child could check the bear's glucose level, which appeared on the monitor, by squeezing one of the buttons embedded in his eight fingers. Jerry was "fed" by passing discs with pictures of different types of foods past his lips, which held a sensor that transmitted the type of food to the monitor in his chest. This allowed a child, before feeding Jerry, to "read" the bear's glucose level by pressing one of the buttons in his fingers. Then, using a stylus, the child "injected" the amount of insulin to balance Jerry's glucose level based on the snack he was about to consume. Jerry still sported the backpack that held the snack discs and stylus.

As Aaron and Hannah worked through the extensive series of prototypes and laid the groundwork for launching their company, their work was facilitated by Betaspring, a Providence, Rhode Island-based start-up accelerator. Betaspring provides mentorship, a small amount of seed capital, legal counsel, and work space for technology and design entrepreneurs. The small-business incubator helped the young founders hone their business model, refine their product, develop a website, and begin the process of building their supply chain. In early 2012, their company was officially established as Sproutel, Inc. The name was derived from the idea of sprouting the imagination of children through story telling.

Initially, they considered offshoring production of Jerry to China. Aaron, in his first-ever trip overseas, visited a number of China factories and held meetings with several companies that had expressed an interest in partnering with him on production. However, after his return to the United States, Aaron noticed that interest from prospective China partners seemed to wane as they refocused on larger customers and new projects that they believed had greater potential. He also came to realize that extending the supply chain to China would slow down product development efforts—always a hurdle for a start-up company. As a poster in the Betaspring offices reads, "The longer it takes to develop, the less likely it is to launch." With this admonition in mind, Aaron and Hannah decided to explore sourcing parts and assembly in the United States.

For the plush bear itself, Aaron looked at a couple of options before settling on the Stuffington Bear Factory, a company based in Phoenix that specializes in the manufacturing of plush toys. The plastic parts for the monitor in Jerry's chest are sourced locally from Rihani, a small injection molding company in Cranston, Rhode Island, and Protomold in Minneapolis. Because of the challenge of finding parts suppliers in the United States, the electronics are still sourced in China. Unfortunately, small start-ups like Sproutel still suffer the consequences of the wholesale offshoring of supply chains over the last twenty-five years.

In order to further localize assembly of Jerry, Sproutel opened an office in the Olneyville section of Providence, a neighborhood that was once a manufacturing center decades ago, fell on tough times, and was struggling to come back. One of the company's goals is to continue to compress their supply chain and source locally whenever possible.

The first official production run of 280 bears was completed in the winter of 2013. Jerry is now being distributed directly to the consumer on the Jerry the Bear website. To spread the word about Jerry, Sproutel exhibits at trade shows and solicits referrals from pediatric endocrinologists and diabetes educators. They are currently working on a partnership with a national health insurance company that would provide Jerry to customers who have children with type 1 diabetes.

What happens to Sproutel after Aaron and Hannah achieve their goal of putting Jerry in the hands of every child with juvenile diabetes? How do they continue to grow? Their business model is to create plush animals to help youngsters with other chronic conditions, such as asthma and autism. As Aaron puts it, "There are, unfortunately, many children that need the help of a friend like Jerry."

Clearly this is a company that balances the need to be a profitable business with the commitment to helping others. For example, on their website, www.jerrythebear.com, consumers can buy a plain plush version of Jerry without the electronics and accessories for measuring glucose levels and administering insulin. The proceeds from the sale of these plain plush bears help to offset the cost of the fully functional Jerry for a diabetic child whose parents cannot afford to buy him. The website even spells out where each dollar goes from the purchase of these fund-raising versions of Jerry.

When asked whether he has any concerns that China manufacturers who have seen the Jerry prototype might steal Sproutel's intellectual property and begin manufacturing and distributing copies of Jerry worldwide, Aaron responds, "Of course, we hope that doesn't come to pass. But if it does, what's the worst that could happen? More children with type 1 diabetes might be helped." Now that's a CEO—and a company—with a social conscience.

As of February 2014, the first production run of bears had sold out, and Jerry had found a permanent home with eighty-seven children like Adam. Eight bears went to nonprofits that use Jerry in group education classes to teach youngsters how to monitor their condition. An ancillary benefit for those who interact with Jerry is that they improve their math skills due to the calculations required to monitor glucose levels and administer insulin. But the biggest benefit of all is the knowledge that you're not alone. As one parent put it, "Some children don't meet anyone else with diabetes for over a year. Knowing that someone else like Jerry has it is an immediate comfort."

The success story of Jerry the Bear and his evolution from design idea to a product that helps children every day is a heartening one. It also proves that any entrepreneur starting up a business and focusing on either a niche market or customizable product should begin his or her sourcing search domestically. Remember that if you want to buy *fewer*, US manufacturers are the best, most cost-effective option.

CHAPTER 5

The Speed Merchants—Moving *Faster*

Use swiftness to wear them out.[78]
The Art of War

On December 1, 2013, Jeff Bezos appeared in a much-publicized CBS News *60 Minutes* segment. The highlight of journalist Charlie Rose's interview was Bezos's revelation that Amazon was exploring the feasibility of using drones to deliver products to its customers. Why drones? To reduce to thirty minutes the time it took from the customer placing an order to actually receiving it. The segment also noted that Amazon continues to build additional distribution centers to get closer to the consumer and ensure quicker delivery. Both the drone project and the proliferation of distribution centers are examples of Amazon's focus on what Bezos calls "customer centricity." Rose described it as "part of what Amazon customers expect—we want it now!"

By April 2015, the US Postal Service had announced that they were experimenting with an eight-rotor drone called the "Horsefly" as a means for speeding up delivery. Similar to an aircraft carrier, a postal van would act as a mobile base for its own fleet of drones. The Horsefly would scan a parcel, use GPS tracking to determine the shortest route to the delivery target, drop the package, and return to the van.[79] Charlie Rose was right; we want it now, and all supply chains will be forced to adapt to this ever more demanding customer imperative.

The need for speed to market reveals a key weakness of most overseas manufacturers—simple geography. Being halfway around the world from your ultimate customer is becoming more and more of a handicap. This was less so during the last half of the twentieth century when the product development cycle was more leisurely and the lowest price trumped all. But a slow boat from China (or Bangladesh or Vietnam) is now too slow, and the unpredictable price of fuel—spurred by volatile oil prices—has raised the cost of transportation to the extent that it narrows the pricing gap between US-made products and imports.

As US manufacturers, we can exploit our geographic advantage by being *faster*. In today's business environment of tighter margins, it is likely that your US prospects and customers currently importing from overseas favor low inventory levels and just-in-time delivery. The best way to accommodate that is to be faster than your competitors, and it is easier and cheaper to be faster when you are nearby. Geographic proximity of supply chain partners and proximity of that supply chain to the ultimate customer are becoming ever more essential for manufacturing success.

The Need for Speed

Why is being *faster* so critical? Because, just as implementing the *fewer* principle takes advantage of the fact that we want exactly what we want, implementing the *faster* principle exploits the fact that we want it *now*—not next week, not tomorrow, but *now*. I was online the other day, and I could not remember the name of the piano player on Miles Davis's *Kind of Blue* album. So I typed in a search, hit the enter button, and over two million results popped up. I clicked on one of those results, and a small circle started to spin around in the tab at the top of my screen. After three seconds, the wait seemed interminable, so I went back and clicked on another result to find the name of jazz pianist Wynton Kelly. Total amount of time to get my answer? Five seconds. But it could have been two seconds if not for the small spinning circle. Admit it; when you're online, if you click on something and that circle spins around on the tab, you become anxious and agitated, don't you? It's because you want your answer *now*—five seconds is too long to wait.

When I was a youngster, if I wanted to know the answer to that same question, I'd have to walk or drive to the nearest record store or library and look up the information. It might have taken me anywhere from one to two hours to get the answer. Yet today, when that circle spins more than three seconds, I'm opting for a different search result or a different screen.

Technology is driving the need for immediacy. It was once predicted that technological improvements would add to our leisure time. In fact, the opposite has occurred because as technology has made us more productive, the time gained has not been converted to leisure time, but time to do more work. We are now busier than we have ever been. So if something takes too long, we don't wait—we move on to the next thing. Our attention span has dissipated.

TV remote controls turned us into channel surfers, focusing on a program for only a few seconds; and if that show doesn't engage or satisfy, we move along to the next channel. Who knows? We might be missing something riveting on one of the other two hundred channels. The development of smartphones and iPads means that we are now digitally connected twenty-four hours a day. When we leave work, we're still working. As a baby boomer, I have always tried to maintain a division between work time and playtime. I do "work things" when I'm working and "play things" when it's playtime, and I have diligently attempted to keep the two from intersecting. Digital technology obliterates that barrier. For younger people who grew up with smartphones, there is little distinction between work time and playtime. Education consultant Marc Prensky memorably defined this distinction between generations as the difference between digital immigrants and digital natives. Largely because of social media, your customers and coworkers are now online friends who are posting twenty-four hours a day. Want to keep up? You'd better stay connected. I'm not saying it's good or bad, only that it is a fact of life. And this technology-driven need for immediacy is becoming hardwired into our mentality.

Don't get me wrong; I'm not complaining. In fact, when it comes to US manufacturing, it's a boon because it opens wide a window of opportunity for US companies. The need to be *faster* will necessarily compress supply chains geographically. If the demand in a particular country is large enough, domestic supply chains will develop in order to more quickly service that market. US manufacturers are fortunate to be sitting in the world's most affluent market, and as people in this country want quicker delivery of consumer products or B2B parts, US-based factories are best positioned to fill that demand. Chinese investors have already recognized the importance of compressing supply chains to attain geographic proximity to the US market. The Keer Group's initial investment of over $200 million in a cotton yarn factory in South Carolina and subsequent plans in 2015 to up the ante with another $65 million is only one of numerous examples.

Time Is Money

Any amount of friction that slows down the speed of a supply chain, whether domestic or global, has a cost; and the cost rises exponentially as the degree of friction rises. The opportunity cost of lost sales, the necessity of financing higher levels of inventory to protect against transportation delays, and the personnel time and effort used to secure alternate sources are only three of the many additional costs associated with supply chain disruptions. And when you offshore to overseas countries, the number of risk factors that impede timely delivery multiply.

Do you think an uncontested election on the other side of the globe would have any bearing on the cost or availability of a T-shirt? In January 2014, the Bangladesh National Party (BNP) boycotted national elections that brought Sheikh Hasina to power. The BNP had hoped that Hasina would step aside before the election and accept neutral oversight of the polling process. She refused and ran unopposed. In January 2015, on the one-year anniversary of the election, the head of the BNP, Khaleda Zia, was planning to lead demonstrations to protest the election that brought Hasina to power. To prevent the demonstrations from taking place, the government placed Zia under virtual house arrest in her party's offices. In response, Zia called for the BNP faithful to blockade roads, rails, and rivers, slowing down or halting apparel shipments from Bangladesh to the United States and other countries. In 2014, Bangladesh exported $4.8 billion of apparel to the United States, ranking third behind China ($29.8 billion) and Vietnam ($9.3 billion). The blockade and resulting supply disruptions sent shock waves through the Bangladeshi economy, as apparel manufacturing accounts for approximately 12 percent of the country's GDP.

The week after the triple disaster of the Japanese earthquake, tsunami, and nuclear meltdown in 2011, the price of certain computer chips used for smartphones, digital cameras, and other devices spiked over 30 percent. Some Japanese auto plants were forced to halt production due to damage from the natural disaster, and the resulting shortage of certain key parts delayed the delivery of some car models to US dealerships.

These types of supply chain disruptions don't happen only in overseas countries. The International Longshore and Warehouse Union (ILWU) represents labor in twenty-nine West Coast ports. Their six-year labor contract with the Pacific Maritime Association, which represents the West Coast carriers and terminals, was set to expire on July 1, 2014. Talks dragged on for months beyond the expiration of the contract, leading to work slowdowns in the winter of 2014 that created massive backlogs of imports on container ships off the West Coast. The strike was eventually settled after federal government intervention, but the backlog of goods bound for factories and stores in the United States took months to dissipate, leaving importers scrambling for alternate sources.

Given the negative impact that such risk factors have on speed to market, many US firms are taking a hard look at their extended supply chains and opting to source at home. In 2009 U.S. Block Windows, a manufacturer based in Pensacola, Florida, decided to reshore production of acrylic blocks. Formerly, the company would ship acrylic resin to China, where it would be molded into blocks for various sizes of residential doors and windows and then shipped back to Pensacola. "With the manufacturing in China, you had to forecast out lead time that with transportation could mean 12 to 14 weeks to delivery," said Roger Murphy, the company's president. "So you were always carrying more inventory than you needed and you also were at risk for being out of something if demand spiked."[80] Six successful years later in 2015, Murphy admitted that he made the decision to reshore less out of patriotism than to protect his bottom line. Given that he reshored at a time when low-cost China imports were flooding the United States, how did reshoring help his bottom line? By increasing his speed to market, he was able to fulfill orders in four production days. The shopworn cliché is truer today than ever before—time is money.

HanesBrands announced in January 2015 that it was expanding its hosiery plant in Clarksville, Arkansas, adding 120 jobs. The plant is one of the largest factories of its kind in the world. Hanes plans to reshore the finishing and packaging of some of its hosiery products. In a press release, Hanes Senior Vice President of Global Operations Javier Chacon explained, "It is not easy for a U.S. plant to compete with offshore competitors, but the capabilities of our plant workforce and management team in Clarksville to continuously adapt, automate and improve efficiency is a testament to the resiliency of this facility since it opened in 1988." The company also noted that some of the key competitive reasons for expanding in Clarksville included the plant's size, the high quality of the hosiery produced there, lower energy costs, and proximity to the US market. In other words, why slow yourself down by manufacturing socks in Arkansas, shipping them overseas for finishing and packaging, then shipping them back to the United States? It takes far too much time—and that's before supply chain risk is factored in.

Thus, the need for speed is compressing supply chains in order to better service the customer. Under Armour's vision for its future manufacturing model is apparent in its new "Project Glory." Their long-term strategy is to manufacture products closer to the markets where they're sold, for instance in the US for US consumers, in Brazil for South American buyers, in Europe for European shoppers and in China for the Chinese market. This would allow them to lessen the amount of obsolete inventory, tailor styles to each market and deliver more quickly to the consumer. Kevin Haley, the company's head of innovation, noted that advanced manufacturing technologies will "reduce lead times and time in transit so the consumer gets what they want more quickly, more efficiently, and gets better products."[81]

After decades of offshoring as a default sourcing position, more US manufacturers are recognizing that a sourcing strategy that may have worked ten years ago is simply too slow today. In the fall of 2014, L. E. K. Consulting interviewed a number of senior US sourcing executives in a variety of manufacturing industries, and one of the key themes they heard time and again was that strong demand from the end buyer, be it a consumer or a B2B purchasing manager, was driving companies to manufacture in closer proximity to their ultimate customer. Key benefits included "greater responsiveness, better positioning in the markets being served and more accurate demand forecasts," as well as more rapid innovation and end-market customization.[82] Note the link between the compression of supply chains and the ability to go *faster* and make *fewer*. Supply chain proximity to the ultimate customer enables greater responsiveness and more rapid innovation (*faster*), as well as end-market customization (*fewer*).

Fast Fashion

For consumers, one of the most prominent examples of the need for speed is the concept of fast fashion. The goal of this business model is to drive apparel sales by getting new fashion designs from catwalk to store rack as quickly as possible at the lowest possible cost. Ideally, this prompts more frequent consumer purchases as stock rotates more quickly into and out of stores. The designs are typically low-priced knockoffs of high-end designer lines. Zara and H&M are two of the many retail chains that have used this model successfully.

In March 2015, an *Atlantic* article noted how fast fashion actually feeds a neurological impulse.[83] We typically experience pleasure with the anticipation of buying something that we desire greatly. However, when it comes time for the actual buying decision, our brain weighs the pleasure of purchasing the desired item against the pain of the price. If the item is greatly desired (let's say, a Givenchy knockoff) and the price is very low, then we experience a higher high. Psychologists call it "transactional utility." If the stock in the stores changes next week, the price is low enough, and you have enough disposable income, you can experience that high all over again. If the stock in the store changes tomorrow, you can get the rush every day.

To make this system work, the supply chain must be able to provide clothing to retailers very quickly. The process from design to sampling to fabric and accessory sourcing to cut and sew operations to store delivery must take place in a matter of weeks, if not days. Since speed is so essential to the process, one might think that fast fashion is a boon for US apparel manufacturers. But let's keep in mind the second piece of the equation, low cost. It's the low price of the goods that allows for the repeat purchases that are the foundation of the business model.

One of the ways fast fashion keeps costs low is through the use of a method known as quick response, first developed by US apparel manufacturers in the 1980s to increase speed to market in response to the competitive threat posed by imports. As apparel manufacturing became more globalized, the principles of quick response were increasingly used to speed up international apparel supply chains, allowing retailers and brands to continue to source from countries with the lowest-cost manufacturers.

One of the criticisms of fast fashion is that it turns apparel into a disposable commodity, stoking consumerism while eating up landfill space. The other, more serious criticism is that the drive to put apparel on store shelves at the lowest possible cost leads to tragedies such as the collapse of the Rana Plaza factory building in Bangladesh. On April 24, 2013, an eight-story commercial building, used primarily for apparel manufacturing, collapsed in the Greater Dhaka Area, killing over 1,100. Apparel headed to prominent retailers such as J. C. Penney and British fashion chain Matalan were discovered in the rubble.[84] This tragedy prompted numerous investigations into supply chains used by major brands and big-box retailers. In April 2015, the United Nation's International Labour Organization reported that over 21 million workers toil in slave-like conditions in factories around the world.[85] The major supply chain culprit? The apparel industry.

The downsides of the fast fashion movement are evident, yet its cachet with consumers is yet another illustration that we are becoming hardwired to want what we want when we want it—even when the consequences can be deadly.

Speed Junkies

One of Trans-Tex's biggest customers in the traditional webbing business had just told me over the phone that they were moving all of their dye sublimation paper sourcing to China. It was 2006, and I had only recently assumed my responsibilities as the company's part-time CEO. Like most small US companies in the textile business, Trans-Tex was already on precarious footing due to the emigration of the industry to China in the race to the bottom on pricing. The defection of this particular customer was a major blow, and it reinforced the importance of moving the company into new markets.

In 2006 Trans-Tex was a slow-footed company. Most of their orders from the traditional webbing business were long-run orders with no particular in-hands date. Because the company had not been compelled to perform quickly, the mind-set was that if something didn't ship today, it could be shipped tomorrow with no consequences.

However, I had set my sights on ramping up the production of lanyards for the promotional products business. This would present a huge cultural hurdle for Trans-Tex. Lead times in that market had been shrinking for two decades, and many promotional products supplier companies—our new target market—were now delivering in a matter of days. Orders for lanyards from these suppliers would have a hard and fast in-hands date because they were generally for a specific event, such as a trade show or walkathon. If they did not arrive on time, the lanyards were useless. Unlike most Trans-Tex orders in the past, when we committed to a ship date, we would have to meet it every time.

A lanyard is a relatively simple product. It consists of a one-yard length of fabric, ranging in width from three-eighths inches to one inch. In the promotional products industry, the webbing is printed with the logo of the company that is ultimately distributing the lanyard. After the webbing is printed, the two ends of the fabric are brought together and formed into a type of necklace by attaching the two ends using sewn thread or a plastic or metal piece that is fitted around the two ends to hold them together. Then the lanyard is ready to accept a name badge holder or other attachments.

Most lanyards, to this day, are assembled by hand. Due to the wide variety of possible attachments, the process is expensive to automate, and no one company has had the critical mass of volume to justify the costs of building custom automation. It is a decidedly old-school manufacturing model for an old-school product. Obviously, the manufacturing of lanyards will never be confused with what is called "advanced manufacturing." One of Phil Barr's friends from the private equity world once toured the

Trans-Tex facility and told him, "You're crazy to be doing this." Perhaps he was right, but one plays the hand that one is dealt.

The relative capabilities of Trans-Tex and the needs of our target market of US promotional products supplier customers dovetailed due to a niche lanyard category—dye sublimated lanyards. Traditionally, 85 to 90 percent of the lanyards sold in the promotional products market had been screen printed. The screen-printing process adds the advertiser's logo to the webbing by simply laying ink through screens directly onto the surface of the lanyard fabric. The webbing is then passed through a heat tunnel that dries the ink onto the fabric.

The chief advantages of the screen-printing process are that it is inexpensive—particularly if the advertiser's logo is only one or two colors—and the process for setting up the artwork allows one to produce very low minimum quantities for a customized order, often as low as fifty units. The significant disadvantage, particularly in the world of promotional products, is that the screen-printing process is not well-suited to laying down multiple colors or complex logos. This meant that most lanyards produced during the '80s and '90s were screen printed with simple block letters. They were sold primarily to smaller local advertisers, schools and trade-show organizers.

The market for lanyards changed after 9/11, when security became a major issue for businesses nationwide. Stiffer security measures were instituted in most corporate offices and production facilities. Included in those security measures was the institution of corporate guidelines requiring employees to present name badges to gain entry. To make it easier to wear and keep track of those corporate ID badges, most companies distributed them on lanyards imprinted with the company's name and/or logo.

Of course, supplier companies recognized this change in the market and jumped into the bourgeoning lanyard category. Remember that most of these supplier companies had already dramatically expanded their product lines by sourcing a wide range of finished goods off the shelves of China factories. So they first tackled the opportunity by importing fully assembled cotton lanyards from China manufacturers, putting them on a warehouse shelf as they did with pens or coffee mugs, and screen printing logos onto them as ordered by distributors.

However, companies increasingly wanted fancier logos or imprints on their lanyards, imprints that could not be accurately reproduced using the screen-printing method. Promotional products suppliers were suddenly receiving an increasing number of lanyard orders with company logos that were too complex—or too expensive—to reproduce using the screen-printing process. Screen printing the word "Microsoft" in block letters in one color is a lot less complicated than reproducing the Microsoft logo itself, with the color gradations in its multicolored four-part flag. Flexography presses like those owned by Trans-Tex were generally required to reproduce these more complex logos. Since flexographic printing for dye sublimation is more expensive than screen printing and since promotional products supplier companies did not own high-speed flexography presses, many supplier companies tackled this problem by sourcing dye sublimated lanyards directly in China. The China manufacturer would both print and assemble the dye sublimated lanyards and ship the completed piece to the supplier or the supplier's customer.

Although delivery was relatively slow and the quality could be marginal, the costs were low out of China, and no investment in people or equipment here in the United States was needed. The long-term problem with this approach was that production lead times for promotional products, as noted previously, were inexorably shrinking. When I began my career with Quill back in 1981, lead times were extended as long as twelve weeks. But by 2005, some suppliers were promoting lead times of five days or less.

This drastic reduction in lead time was enabled by the change in the supplier business model from manufacturing to importing/decorating. Most promotional products suppliers after 2000 were importing unprinted, or what is commonly called "blank," products from China manufacturers, storing the products in their warehouses here in the United States, and simply pulling the product off the shelf and screen printing a logo onto it when they received an order. However, dye sublimated lanyards were a different story. Since they were custom printed before being assembled into a final product, it wasn't possible to store a blank lanyard on a shelf and then dye sublimation print it, as could be done with screen printing. It had to be printed *before* assembly. Thus, China manufacturers were both printing and assembling the dye sublimated lanyards, which created complications in terms of lead time.

Because of the extended lead times out of China, some suppliers began to explore options for producing dye sublimation lanyard orders domestically. They soon discovered, however, that the high-speed flexography presses (like those owned by Trans-Tex) required to print dye sublimation paper were far too expensive to buy and operate given the number of lanyard orders received on a yearly basis requiring dye sublimation printing. Some researched the feasibility of buying short-run digital presses and converting them to print dye sublimation inks instead of standard inks. This allowed them to introduce dye sublimation printed lanyards as a standard product in their catalogs. However, because they could only be assembled after the webbing was printed, lead times were longer than for most promotional products.

Another complication was that Fortune 500 companies typically needed significantly more lanyards than the local high school or community bank. However, because digital short-run presses operate so slowly, if a supplier received an order for 25,000 lanyards for a larger company, printing the required paper would tie up those relatively slow digital dye sublimation printers for literally days at a time. This would force suppliers to turn down orders for smaller quantities and disappoint some of their best repeat customers, because they did not have enough dye sublimation printing capacity on the slow, short-run digital presses. They were able to produce smaller quantities with high-quality imprints, but if they accepted a larger order, it would be to the detriment of their normal flow of smaller orders.

Meanwhile, back at Trans-Tex in Providence, I had set my sights on these lanyard suppliers as potential customers. Since they owned only slower, short-run digital presses and Trans-Tex had plenty of capacity on our high-speed flexography presses, the opportunity clearly existed for Trans-Tex to handle the longer-run dye sublimation lanyard orders that suppliers were currently turning away or sending to China.

At Trans-Tex we had successfully sold dye sublimated lanyards, in a very limited way, to one small promotional products supplier in the Northeast, so I was convinced our business model of selling through those types of companies could work. The big questions were whether we had the capability to do it successfully for multiple suppliers on a grander scale and whether we could do it quickly enough to satisfy the need for speed to market. Trans-Tex was still a relatively small company, and with the standard production lead time for promotional products orders having plummeted down to five production days or less, we would have little margin for error. If we did not ship these lanyard orders on time and with the high-quality printing that advertisers had come to expect, we would fumble away our greatest growth opportunity. However, I remained convinced that orders would follow if we could prove our business model worked.

Our first order of business was to establish hard and fast production lead times on all lanyard orders. I knew that Trans-Tex could not match China factories on price. The price for dye sublimated lanyards from China was generally one third lower than our price. But I also knew that if we could produce faster than China that we could beat them. In 2006, our China competitors were landing dye sublimated lanyards into the United States in three to four weeks. So we set lead times at ten working days for orders with new artwork and five working days for repeat orders. Because our minimum order size at the time was 2,500 units and above—which was a relatively large order for the promotional products business—this was an aggressive lead time given the company's past service level. However, when implementing the *faster* principle, the first and most important step is to benchmark your overseas competition's lead times, establish your lead times significantly below theirs, and then find a way to do it. If you do the reverse and try to find a way to produce *faster* before establishing quicker lead times, odds are that you'll never make it happen. You must drive a stake in the ground first.

As with implementing the *fewer* principle, we became *faster* largely due to the quality of our team. Keep in mind that the assembly process could not be automated. But that did not prevent us from being *faster*. When we embarked on the lanyard journey, I began to hire key people who once worked with me at Quill. Because they already understood the promotional products distribution network, they knew the challenges we would face and had learned at Quill the sense of urgency that would be required. They were also battle tested under the conditions of tight lead times and little margin for error. We also had an operations manager, Bob Laferriere, who had a bit of a chip on his shoulder after watching his father's business decimated by the offshoring of the US textile business to China. He had a score to settle. Never forget that if you want your company to be *faster*, the first ingredient is people who care.

One year later, we were hitting all of our lead-time marks. It didn't require the introduction of lean manufacturing principles or the installation of top-of-the-line automation. The company's primary investment to that point had been in people and in a bigger facility to handle the higher flow of lanyard orders. There was some investment in basic assembly equipment, heat transfer machines, and computers, but those outlays scaled with the increase in business.

We had hit our stride by late summer 2009. One of our best new lanyard customers was in the sports marketing business, selling lanyards to most of the professional sports teams, major colleges, and souvenir shops. In October they sent us a tentative order for 2,500 lanyards to be made and distributed at a hospitality event in New York if the Yankees won the American League Championship Series against the Los Angeles Angels. The lanyards would carry the Major League Baseball logo and read "World Series 2009." They needed to be at Yankee Stadium for the event by noon on Tuesday, October 27. But the series was not decided until a Yankee victory in game seven late on Sunday evening, October 25. This left Trans-Tex thirty-six hours to custom print, assemble, and deliver the product. On Tuesday morning at 8:30 a.m., a driver loaded the custom-made lanyards into his car and left Trans-Tex for the Bronx. An overseas manufacturer had no chance of making and delivering that order. But Trans-Tex could and did. That's when I knew we were ready for the next step.

As noted in the last chapter, our investment in short-run digital presses in late 2009 enabled us to make *fewer*. Our minimum order size for lanyards quickly dropped from 2,500 to 250. If our China competitors were having a tough time competing against us on large orders of 2,500 or more, they would have little to no chance of beating us on 250-piece orders, particularly since, by then, we had dropped our production lead time to five working days on orders with new artwork. Even given their significant pricing advantage per piece, a China manufacturer could not produce 250 units of a customized lanyard and have it in the US customer's hand in five working days without sending it here via air freight, a costly proposition.

Since the average order size for a promotional products supplier is only about $650, our reduction in the minimum order size opened up a much broader market, and as noted previously, the order count jumped substantially. And so did revenue. Even during the depths of the Great Recession, the business continued to grow. By 2012 we had outgrown our second facility and moved to a new location in Cranston, Rhode Island.

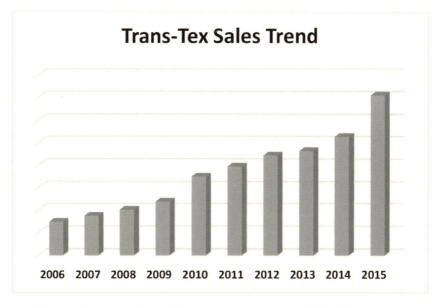

The left axis is purposely blank. Because it is a privately-held company, actual Trans-Tex sales volume is confidential information.

But one final *faster* challenge lay ahead. Our biggest lanyard customer asked if we could provide twenty-four-hour turn time on orders. For years, the lead time in the promotional products industry had been shrinking, and most of the larger supplier companies were offering twenty-four-hour service on many of their product lines. However, for Trans-Tex, this presented a unique challenge. No supplier company had aggressively marketed a twenty-four-hour turn on dye sublimated lanyards, precisely because the process was more labor intensive than simply screen printing a logo on a coffee mug. Also, the number of twenty-four-hour orders we were likely to get would be relatively small, yet the only way we could provide twenty-four-hour service was by running at least two shifts and a skeleton shift overnight as a third shift. Clearly, in order to guarantee twenty-four-hour service, we would need to keep the order pipeline full so that second and third shift team members were fully occupied.

We decided to gamble on the proposition that if we built the capacity, the orders would come. Since no supplier had aggressively marketed twenty-four-hour turn on dye sublimated lanyards, we calculated that there must be pent-up demand for the service. We staffed the necessary shifts and committed to a twenty-four-hour turn for our biggest customer on any order for one thousand pieces or less within a broad set of parameters. The capability was launched in January 2014, and the orders did indeed come. During some months, the percentage of orders requiring twenty-four-hour turn was as high as 30 percent. The higher service level also seemed to spur a general increase in our customers' sales of dye sublimated lanyards regardless of the lead time, so the pipeline filled. Being *faster* once again created a spike in our business.

As with our initial entry into the lanyard business and the decision to begin producing smaller orders, people were the key to making it work. We did buy several next-generation digital presses that were faster and produced higher print quality. Also, as noted in the last chapter, we invested in technology that allowed us to import orders from our biggest customers directly into our IT system. This allowed us to more quickly enter orders without a significant increase in personnel. We also launched an incentive program to keep our team's focus on ensuring that every twenty-four-hour turn order was shipped on time. But the team's commitment to making it work was the essential element in our success.

Why is the Trans-Tex story so relevant to the *faster* principle? Because it illustrates that even a company in a very basic industry can implement the *faster* principle and dramatically increase the odds for success against overseas competition. Automation is, of course, another way to become *faster*. But many smaller companies either cannot afford automation, or like Trans-Tex, their product does not lend itself to automated assembly. Programs like Six Sigma, based on a lean manufacturing model, can also make a company much *faster*. But the game isn't over if you don't have the money to pay a Six Sigma consultant. Smaller cash-strapped manufacturers should not wring their hands and succumb to the idea that only government programs and policies will save them from global competition. Because becoming *faster* is, first of all, a mind-set. Start with that mind-set and drive your *faster* stake in the ground.

Never forget that delivering precisely when the customer wants will forge a powerful bond between you and your customer. When your company is the path of least resistance for a customer's orders, business will continue to flow out of sheer momentum. If your lead time is "whenever the customer wants it," your overseas competitors can, at best, only equal that performance; they cannot surpass it.

CHAPTER 6

The Best in Class—Manufacturing *Finer*

> When you see a gap, then advance.[86]
> *The Art of War*

When Raelynn Hughes of Holland, Michigan, founded her company, Mommy Necklaces, in 2004, overseas competition was not even on her radar screen. Raelynn's goals were safety, fashion, and comfort. As a young mother with a new baby, she noticed that her easily distracted breast-feeding daughter, Megan, would instantly calm down when she focused on the heirloom necklace that Raelynn had received as a gift from her grandmother. The baby would hold it, twist it, and try to put it in her mouth. Raelynn was naturally concerned that her baby might accidentally break the necklace or that the jewelry might contain metals that would be harmful to her child. So she went to her computer and scanned stores that sold baby toys, trying to find a safe and practical substitute for her grandmother's necklace. *It would be nice if it was also fashionable and relatively inexpensive, too,* she thought. She quickly discovered that there was nothing available.

Then and there Mommy Necklaces was born. Now a thriving company, with a wide range of safety-tested products, Mommy Necklaces distributes in the United States and overseas. Her product contains no harmful chemicals or toxins, cording with a breakaway closure and beads that will not break, splinter, or crack under the regular duties of motherhood. Hughes has made a commitment to remain US-sourced. She tests all components for product safety and guarantees to repair any of her necklaces that are broken—no matter how.

Hughes employs a number of young women in the area, many of whom discovered the company as new mothers. They work on production of the final product either at the Mommy Necklaces design studio or by taking pieces home to assemble. As she describes it, "There is no sweat shop, child labor, or assembly line. We're a puzzle of perfection that could not be put together with the same integrity if we were outsourced and were disconnected from our sources."[87]

Ms. Hughes decided that all cords, components, and beads would be sourced in the United States because she wanted to support manufacturing in this country. She chose as her supplier of beads the Greene Plastics Company in Hope Valley, Rhode Island. Around this time she would read news reports about recalls of imported products due to excessive lead or phthalate content. Greene Plastics continuously tested its beads to ensure they were within standards set by the Consumer Products Safety Commission (CPSC).

"From the beginning," Ms. Hughes recounted in a 2012 interview, "I wasn't trying to scare people, but simply open their eyes to the magnitude of this potential problem. Our customers could buy our products with complete confidence that it was safe for their baby to be around our jewelry without worry that a transfer of toxic chemicals could occur."[88] Her focus on the safety issue when she first started the company in 2004 would prove prescient.

Tipping the Scales

As imports from low-wage countries flooded the US market during the last twenty-five years, dramatic changes in US product safety regulations, largely driven by high-profile stories of lead-tainted toys imported from China, have exposed weaknesses in the overseas manufacturing business model. This has opened a window of opportunity for US manufacturers. By refocusing our manufacturing operations on improving in two key areas—product safety and quality—we ensure a happy customer experience. As the pricing gap between imported products and our manufactured goods continues to narrow, being a *finer* company is the third attribute, along with *fewer* and *faster*, of an American Dragon. It will tip the scales in your favor when your US customer or prospect is making the final buying decision.

Pricing for *Finer*

In 2004, the same year that Raelynn Hughes was starting her company, Mommy Necklaces, the California Department of Public Health began distributing 300,000 lunch boxes to children throughout the state to promote eating fresh fruits and vegetables. One third of those were supplied by TA Creations, a Los Angeles company that had imported the products from China. Two years later, a spot check by a Sacramento County lab discovered that some of those lunch boxes contained lead levels significantly above the legal limit prescribed by California Proposition 65—at that time six hundred parts per million. All 300,000 lunch boxes were recalled, and TA Creations was eventually slapped with a $10 million fine, the largest legal judgment against an offender up to that time. This was only the opening salvo in a barrage of product safety news that would begin the inexorable process that now seriously weakens our overseas competition.

Keep in mind that when imports decimated US manufacturers in the '80s and '90s, the widespread differential in price was the predominant driver in the marketplace. Certainly the quality of product coming from China factories was, in general, far below that coming from US manufacturers, but the price differential was so great that most US corporate buyers and consumers were willing to sacrifice quality in favor of their budget.

At Quill in the 1980s, we were competing against a small coterie of other US-made pen brands selling at similar price points. Analyzing the relative features and benefits of my own company's product and crafting a marketing message to compete with them was relatively simple. In a much smaller sense, it was a situation similar to the Big Three automakers here in the United States before Japanese imports flooded the market; although we competed aggressively, the market was more than big enough for all of us. We could coexist taking our yearly single-to-double digit sales increases and repeating the process the following year. This approach worked reasonably well for me at Quill, as it did for the Big Three Detroit automakers, until the world changed.

By the time the 90s rolled around, Quill's unique design had been knocked off by several China manufacturers, and cheap imports began flooding the US market. We continued to manufacture a far better product than those imitations, and I was certain that as we continued to pound home our US-made quality and lifetime guarantee, most of our customers would eschew the cheap Chinese knockoffs. It was a grave miscalculation. In retrospect, my presumption that our customer base would continue to buy from us out of loyalty to US manufacturing was naïve. The price differential was simply so great that it trumped both the level of our quality and the fact that our pens were made in the United States of America *and* featured a lifetime guarantee. It taught me a lesson I'll never forget: relying solely on the patriotism of your customer to keep you in business is a vain hope, not a reliable business model.

As the new millennium began, Quill, like most US manufacturers, had capitulated and begun sourcing many of its newer pen models from China. And there were many other companies like us.

Atchison Products was a canvas tote bag manufacturer founded in 1908 in Atchison, Kansas. Their story is like that of many other small to midsize manufacturers, who slowly but steadily grew over several decades, providing jobs for those in the local community. As the '90s progressed, they stubbornly refused to offshore production and suffered serious sales erosion due to the price differential with their competitors importing bags from China. Ultimately, they began shopping in China and launched an import line that halted the slow downward spiral. By 2005 sales had recovered to approximately $15 million, and they continued to employ 125 people in the Atchison area, largely decorating imported bags with custom logos for the promotional products market. In 2006, the company was sold to BIC Graphic USA, a division of the manufacturer of the ubiquitous plastic stick pen, and the Atchison operation was shuttered and moved to Florida.

The Atchison story, like that of Quill, illustrates that even those manufacturers stubbornly pulling against the tide of lower-quality imports eventually were forced to surrender in order to remain in business. When competing with US importers bringing in products that cost 30 to 50 percent less than their own domestically produced goods, the owners and managers of small US manufacturers were faced with the stark choice of the slow death of their companies or joining the parade of US buyers shopping overseas for low-priced, mediocre-quality imports.

Headlining for *Finer*

As that parade of US buyers trooping to China lengthened, the passage of California Proposition 65 in 1986 was a harbinger of dramatic changes in the product safety landscape; and those changes became one part of the equation that would subtly shift the macroeconomic manufacturing landscape in favor of small to midsize US manufacturers. With the passage of Proposition 65, for the first time, businesses were prohibited from knowingly exposing consumers to potentially dangerous substances without clearly notifying them of the presence of those substances. The burden of proof was placed on companies, not government, to ensure that they were selling products that complied with official limits on hazardous chemicals.

This was clearly a challenge for US manufacturers, who now had to comply with a more stringent set of safety regulations in California than in the rest of the country. It was an even greater challenge for US companies importing finished goods. Many of these importers had been simply shopping product off the shelf of a trade show booth of a China manufacturer or agent in Hong Kong. They may have never taken the time to actually visit the factory where the products were manufactured. They never inspected the materials going into the products they were importing from China and never saw the conditions in the factories. They were buying from China like one would buy a can of peas off the shelf of a grocery store and simply assuming the imported products were safe.

But Proposition 65 forced importers to pay more careful attention to the "DNA" of a product—the base metal from which it was constructed, the chemicals that were used to manufacture it, the composition of the paint that decorated it. Although these were also challenges for small to midsize domestic manufacturers, they were far more onerous challenges for an importer with little knowledge or control of a manufacturing process taking place half a world away. Of course, if you were an importer not willing to comply, you could choose to stop selling into California, or you could cross your fingers, continue business as usual, and risk heavy fines.

Three years after the TA Creations lunch box controversy, on June 19, 2007, the *New York Times* reported that all of the twenty-four toys recalled by the Consumer Products Safety Commission since the beginning of that year had been manufactured in China, including 1.5 million Thomas and Friends trains and rail components.[89] Two months later, Mattel recalled one million toys—all manufactured in China—due to excessive lead levels. The recall covered eighty-three products, including Sesame Street and Nickelodeon characters. These high-profile recalls created much controversy in consumer product safety circles and grabbed the attention of the media, federal and state legislators, and the Consumer Products Safety Commission.

Largely as a result of that uproar, roughly one year later on August 14, 2008, President George W. Bush signed the new Consumer Products Safety Improvement Act (CPSIA). Between 2002 and 2007, the number of recalls of products made in China doubled, and the law was a direct response to those recalls, particularly those related to the above-mentioned children's products tainted with lead paint. The new law banned all products with a lead content of more than six hundred parts per million by February 2009 and drastically reduced the allowable level of lead content in any children's product to one hundred parts per million by February 2011. The law also banned the manufacture, distribution, and sale of any child care product that contained concentrations of more than 0.1 percent of phthalates, a compound that previously had been used in a number of plastic products, including some drinking containers.

Finally, the new law set up strict testing requirements to ensure compliance, including a paper trail in the form of a general conformity certificate (GCC) that would compel a US distributor of an imported product to document and have available the ultimate manufacturing source. Thus, importers are now required to have on file a record of an imported product's "DNA," including the date and place where the product was manufactured and the date and place where the product was tested. One look at the form (see below) drives home that this created a significant hurdle for importers of products from China; it was good news for US manufacturers trying to win back US customers and prospects from China.

Sample General Certificate of Conformity - Mattress*

1. **Identification of the product covered by this certificate:**
   Luxe Mattress Models #456, 789 (Queen, King)

2. **Citation to each CPSC product safety regulation to which this product is being certified:**
   16 CFR Part 1632, Standard for the Flammability of Mattresses and Mattress Pads
   16 CFR Part 1633, Standard for the Flammability (Open Flame) of Mattress Sets

3. **Identification of the U.S. importer or domestic manufacturer certifying compliance of the product:**
   Mattress Safety USA Importers
   123 Good Sleep Way
   Springfield, MA 12345
   (549) 456-7890

4. **Contact information for the individual maintaining records of test results:**
   Mary Smith, Compliance and Quality Control
   Mattress Safety USA Importers
   123 Good Sleep Way
   Springfield, MA 12345
   (549) 456-7890 ext. 99, mary@mattresssafety101.net

5. **Date and place where this product was manufactured:**
   May 2011, Guangzhou, China

6. **Date and place where this product was tested for compliance with the regulation(s) cited above:**
   June 2011
   Guangzhou, China

7. **Identification of an accredited laboratory accepted by the CPSC on whose testing the certificate depends:**
   Guangzhou Quality Labs
   No. 023 Shi Nan Road
   Dong Zhou, Pan Zi
   Guangzhou City
   Guangdong Province, China 511453

In this example, while the mattresses were not required to be tested by a third party laboratory, the mattress manufacturer voluntarily chose to do so and must provide the information about that laboratory. If you do not use a third party laboratory, you may label this section "N/A." If the mattresses being certified are for cribs or children's size mattresses, please see the requirements for issuing a CPC.

*From Consumer Products Safety Commission Website

Blindsiding China

Unilife, which manufactures prefilled syringes with retractable needles for the health care market, moved jobs back from China to a plant in York, Pennsylvania, primarily to ensure compliance with FDA regulations. Alan Shortall, Unilife's CEO, stated in a June 2012 *Bloomberg News* report that "The very thing in the U.S.A. that oftentimes we complain about—the complexity of the rules and the regulations—works for us. FDA compliance is the main reason we're here."[90] It is not unusual for small to midsize US companies to have a knee-jerk negative reaction against any government regulation. However, if you are competing directly with overseas manufacturers, tighter product safety regulations can be your friend. Even some larger companies have reshored jobs precisely because of stringent CPSC or FDA rules.

One only needs to read the news to know that many Asian manufacturers have exhibited little to no understanding of the importance of product safety in the United States. And it is not as though they are dumping unsafe, inferior product only on unsuspecting consumers here in the States. Rather, it is a pattern of behavior that proves that lax safety standards are both tolerated and even covered up at some of the highest corporate levels.

During the height of the 2008 US recalls of lead-tainted toys manufactured in China, executives at the Sanlu Group, China's largest producer of powdered milk, discovered that some of their products were laced with melamine, a chemical used to produce plastic and fertilizer. It was apparently added to the milk powder to boost the measurable protein content of the product. However, with the Beijing Olympics due to begin in a matter of days, the company opted to bury the news for five weeks to prevent an embarrassing revelation during the Games and continued to sell the product for consumption by infants.[91] Six babies died from kidney stones and other kidney damage, and over eight hundred were hospitalized. Two people were eventually executed, another given a suspended death sentence, and three received a sentence of life imprisonment. So one would think this would be the end of the possibility of finding melamine in powdered milk in China.

Yet in late 2010 and early 2011, packets of melamine-tainted powdered milk were again found on store shelves in China. Incredibly, some of the product seized during the 2008 scandal had been reused and put back on retail shelves three years later.[92] In July 2012 state media outlets announced that more contaminated formula was discovered in Guangzhou, China. Tests confirmed that the formula contained excessive amounts of the carcinogen aflatoxin. This was only one month after baby formula with dangerous levels of mercury had been discovered.[93]

In his book *The End of Cheap China*, Shaun Rein (no "China basher" by any means) recounts that after the tainted milk scandal resurfaced in 2011, the Chinese government shut down 50 percent of the dairies because officials were still finding traces of melamine in dairy products. The government arrested two thousand and closed 4,900 businesses, yet Rein comments that this "is likely a small drop in the bucket because the problems are so immense."[94]

These episodes, and many others like them, clearly illustrate that there is a systemic flaw in product and food safety monitoring in China, a flaw that we can and should exploit when competing with China manufacturers.

Testing for *Finer*

In order to solidify their relationship with one of their largest US customers, Trans-Tex initiated a process of regular quality and safety testing. The product they provided to this customer was safety straps used to hold young children in shopping carts, so the tensile strength of the webbing was critical. Carts often sit for hours in the direct sunlight, and fading of the straps from exposure to the sun's ultraviolet rays is also a concern. Although the customer had routinely tested for the strap's tensile strength, Trans-Tex began investing in their own twice-yearly tensile strength tests with the local division of a multinational product safety lab, UL. They also began date coding each production run so that used webbing could be traced back to its date of manufacture.

While the tensile strength tests were being done, Trans-Tex also invested in colorfastness tests at intervals of one hundred hours to five hundred hours in conditions that approximated direct exposure to UV rays. This allowed them, as supplier and customer, to establish the first set of measurable standards for ultraviolet protection on the straps. Prior to that, quality had been defined in a purely subjective manner, without hard data. Even more importantly, it illustrated to this customer that they were willing to invest in product testing to ensure the success of both companies. Trans-Tex became the go-to source by implementing consistent internal quality standards.

Capitol Cups in Auburn, Alabama, maker of stadium-style plastic cups, insulated cups, and children's "sippy" cups, is one of the few, if not the only, US manufacturer of plastic-insulated children's cups still standing after years of low-cost China imports flooded the market. Capitol has taken advantage of the news reports of BPA-tainted plastic products from China and their own production innovations to secure a place on Walmart's shelves. Streamlining the production process down to a single molding machine instead of four has allowed Capitol to *undercut* import prices while still providing a product to US consumers that is safety-tested to meet Consumer Product Safety Commission standards.

Exploit this weakness in the overseas manufacturing model by investing in regular product safety testing, if required for the types of products you manufacture. If product safety testing is not required for your products, consider testing for other voluntary quality standards to use as part of your sales and marketing message to US customers currently buying overseas. This commitment sets benchmarks against which you can be objectively measured by your customer, strengthens the relationship with that customer by illustrating your commitment to quality and safety, and raises the bar for both your foreign and domestic competition. To take that business back from you, your competitors will be forced to invest in similar quality/safety testing and show a commitment to hitting measurable benchmarks over the long term simply to get back in the game.

When it is time to talk about product safety issues with your US customer or prospect currently buying overseas, do not hesitate to actively plant doubt in their mind, not only about whether the quality of the product they are ordering is adequate, but also whether the product is CPSIA compliant. Collect and use copies of newspaper articles about product recalls that highlight this shortcoming. There is nothing wrong with selling fear, especially if that fear is well-founded and well-documented. After all, if a China manufacturer will sell lead-tainted toys to Mattel and melamine-laced powdered milk to a child, what might they sell to a small US importer/customer with no eyes on the manufacturing process in China?

Imagine if your US customer, to whom you sold imported product, walks out of his or her office one day and is confronted by *60 Minutes* correspondent Steve Kroft. He shoves a microphone in the customer's face and asks whether he or she knows that the products he or she is currently importing have twice the allowable CPSC lead limits and whether he or she understands the danger this poses to children. There is simply no graceful way to deal with such a scenario. And if you are the vendor who sold them the product, it can kill your business.

How do you remain informed of the ongoing changes in the product safety landscape? If your marketplace has a nonprofit trade association, that is the best place to start. Such organizations typically follow and publish relevant product safety news in their trade journals or on their website. Some have web-based applications that allow one to determine whether a particular product is subject to product safety regulations and what type of documentation or testing is required.

One of the best such sites is sponsored by Promotional Products Association International (PPAI). Many products in that marketplace are imported, so distributors and buyers are particularly concerned about whether the products they are buying comply with all relevant safety guidelines. Their "Turbo Test" application is a product safety road map that guides the user step-by-step through a process that identifies the appropriate compliance testing and standards required for literally thousands of products.

Rick Brenner, a prominent blogger on product compliance issues and former chairman of the board of PPAI, agrees that a trade association can be a valuable resource. However, Brenner also recommends, once you have determined your product is subject to Consumer Product Safety Commission guidelines, that you contact a good product safety attorney and initiate regular reviews—either quarterly or semiannually—to discuss:

1. What has changed in your business that involves product safety regulations?

2. What will change in the regulatory environment that might affect your business?
3. What potential product compliance issues are down the road?

Product safety compliance is the primary way for you to differentiate your company from your overseas competition. But a *finer* company must also routinely deliver a quality product. Over the course of the last thirty years, as overseas manufacturers ate into our market share here in the United States, we lost our way to varying degrees from a quality standpoint. Competing almost exclusively on price due to the onslaught of cheap imported goods, we generally let product quality slide in order to hit a price point and to ensure the survival of our companies. However, as the price of goods from countries such as China continues to rise, an opportunity opens up to provide better quality than they can produce while maintaining competitive pricing. Meanwhile, most of those countries struggling to take market share from China do not have the manufacturing expertise or infrastructure to provide better quality than China and still keep costs low. With the pendulum of China pricing swinging in the opposite direction, now is the time for US manufacturers to renew our commitment to quality.

Benchmark your overseas competition and make objectively measurable distinctions between your product quality and theirs, particularly if product safety compliance is involved. Emphasize those distinctions as a key part of your sales and marketing message to those US prospects you are trying to win or win back.

Trusting for *Finer*

Being a finer company also means that your US customer trusts you to not sell around them to their customer. One of the most disruptive effects of the technology/globalization vortex is that it is now easier than ever for an overseas manufacturer to locate their US importer's customers and, either purposely or inadvertently, sell around them. This has happened in a number of marketplaces, but the apparel business is a clear example. Disintermediation in the US textile business has been succinctly described by Ram Sareen, an executive at TUKATECH, a California-based apparel technology firm and a member of the Americas Apparel Producers Network. In an e-mail distributed to members of the network in January 2010, Sareen wrote:

> The offshore factories that can export directly to U.S. retailers are already contacting retailers here to work directly with them; they are securing their own position for the long run. In California, I have seen China-based exporters hiring designers and calling directly on retailers to offer their own designs, but with better terms and prices by eliminating middlemen, driving (U.S.) importers out of business.

He goes on to state that apparel brands first sent manufacturing offshore and then design and development. Now that control over design, development, and manufacturing has been ceded to China, the Internet will allow China sources to control distribution. Sareen's prediction is that there will eventually be direct-to-consumer Internet sales of apparel from Asia to Main Street, USA. They have the cash to fund it, and the US consumer has been focused almost exclusively on getting the lowest price, using the Internet to bypass traditional distribution networks. Who made this possible? According to Sareen, it was "U.S. importing companies who brought goods in, sent money out and empowered the very (overseas) factories who now have the wherewithal to leverage the internet like never before."

This is the same Trojan horse scenario that confronts suppliers in the promotional products distribution network. In the 1980s most of the suppliers in that marketplace were manufacturers selling to distributors, who were then reselling to corporate buyers. But as low-priced China imports flooded into the United States, many of those suppliers shut down or curtailed their manufacturing operations and began expanding their product lines by buying product off the shelf from China manufacturers. As their business grew and their overseas sources came to realize the size of the market, some China manufacturers and exporters began to sell around their US supplier customers directly to the distributors. Some are now also selling around the distributors and directly to the advertiser if the order size is large enough.

Clearly, this is an ominous development for US importers and distributors of China-made product. The reality—and even the threat—of China manufacturers selling around their US customer is a weakness in their business model that you can exploit. As the Internet makes marketplaces more transparent, trustworthiness becomes more vital to your customers and prospects. If your US customer or prospect is concerned that their overseas source may sell around them, it opens the door for you to exploit this fear by demonstrating to them that you will maintain the integrity of their distribution network even if it means a short-term loss.

Trans-Tex could easily generate higher margins by selling around one of their most important customers, Dayton Products. Because Trans-Tex acts as a silent manufacturing partner, they typically "blind ship" directly to this customer's customers. These ultimate customers do not even know that Trans-Tex exists, yet we have contact information, in the form of shipping addresses, for all of them. It would be relatively easy to set up a company under another name and solicit the business directly from those ultimate customers, concentrating on the largest. Indeed, it is not atypical for some overseas manufacturers to do precisely that.

How long would it be before Internet transparency exposed this backdoor ploy and Trans-Tex lost the customer that originally brought them this large chunk of business? This betrayed customer would tell others throughout the distribution network, and eventually Trans-Tex would be trusted by no one. Perhaps they would have generated higher margins over the short term, but at a loss of potentially greater long-term revenue from a steadily growing customer.

Another way that a *finer* company builds trust with a US prospect to win them back—or to prevent them from going overseas—is to develop relationships between your company and your customers and prospects at several levels in the respective organizations. At Trans-Tex, a total of seven employees from different departments visited Dayton Products to get a better sense of this customer's operation and to develop multiple relationships at different levels within the two companies. This pays dividends when challenges arise that require a quick resolution or the involvement of a multidisciplinary team.

You should encourage these types of intercompany visits from people in various departments of your operation, particularly those who communicate regularly by phone or e-mail with your customer. Your sales team should not be the only people hitting the road to visit key accounts. The relationship between members of your customer service team and the order processing department of your customer is critical to the smooth and timely processing of orders. Bring as many of your customer service team members as possible to visit that customer and encourage their order processing team members to visit you. Budgetary constraints can limit this exchange, but one or two people exchanging such visits is always better than no effort at all. These relationships at different levels throughout the two organizations strengthen the bonds between your two companies and increase the level of trust. It is also something that your China competition is unlikely to do.

Committing to *Finer*

Another aspect of being a finer company is your commitment to the customer's order not only during the manufacturing process, but also before the order is sent to the factory floor. As noted in our discussion of the *faster* principle, there is now precious little time between your receipt of the order and the ship date. Every hour is important. Thus, your customer service team must be highly proactive to ensure that you have all of the information you need to put an order into production. This means more than making a phone call or sending an e-mail to seek clarification and then dropping the order into a "pending" bin. The customer service team must return to those unprocessed orders once or twice a day, touching base with the customer again to solicit the necessary information. It must be made clear to that customer that until you receive all of the information you need to process the order, it will remain in limbo.

At Trans-Tex, our customer service team is so experienced and knows the marketplace, their customers, and their order habits so well that they serve as a secondary order entry proofing department for larger customers, often catching errors that a foreign source would simply pass into production. For example, one order repeated occasionally, but each successive order had a slight variation in the finished product. A new order entry person at the customer's office did not recognize that this slight variation was the norm and simply asked for an exact repeat of the previous order. This immediately raised a red flag at Trans-Tex, and they called back to clarify the purchase order, explain the process to the customer's order entry person, and retrieve the information needed for the customized variation. In essence, the Trans-Tex customer service person was training their customer's order entry team.

This proactive approach will often get your customer out of a jam. Perhaps they lost track of the order, or an experienced team member at their end is out sick for the day. By contacting the customer on a regular basis for information on pending orders and double-checking when the information on an order seems out of the ordinary, you will not annoy them; rather, you will prove to them your commitment to quickly, efficiently, *and* correctly processing their orders. Meanwhile, their Asian source is often dealing with a roughly nine- to twelve-hour lag time in communication due to the difference in time zones.

Since accurate order processing is so critical to great customer service, the language barrier is another weakness that you can exploit. Cultural nuances, spelling and grammar issues, and the above-mentioned time difference make clarifying order information and resolving disputes with an Asian source a timely and complicated process. This is not only a *finer* issue, but also a *faster* issue. If your team is in constant contact with your customer over issues such as order clarification, projected ship dates, and problem resolution, you will save your customer time and money in ways that your Asian competition cannot.

On the subject of dispute resolution, the crowning attribute of a *finer* company is post-sale commitment to customer satisfaction. Many US importers have been blindsided by overseas manufacturers who do not stand behind their product if there are defects. Most Asian sources require a substantial portion of the value of the order paid up front. If your US customer or prospect has a quality problem with the delivered product, it can be difficult to resolve the issue in their favor. Once they buy it, they own it unless they have substantial leverage with the source.

To exploit this weakness, a *finer* company must always give the US customer the benefit of the doubt. If responsibility for a defect or other error is in a gray area between you and your customer, accept responsibility, fix or replace the product quickly, and move on. Your overseas competitor will rarely provide that type of post-sale commitment. Be prepared to talk the talk *and* walk the walk. Tell your US prospects currently buying from overseas that they can trust you—and then prove it.

Walking the Walk

Raelynn Hughes at Mommy Necklaces continues to fight the battle with imports every day. The cheap imported knockoffs are a constant threat, but her customers trust her and the safety of her products. Occasionally, mothers of young children who buy her necklaces will send her some of their old jewelry, and subsequent testing will reveal lead levels far above the legal limit.

"Moms stop wearing jewelry because they are fearful it will break," Hughes relates. "But what most Moms don't realize is that this is not the only concern. Most everyday jewelry is loaded with toxic levels of metals. We test it regularly and the results are often scary. It's ironic that we think about what we feed our kids, what chemicals are in the diapers, environmental toxins in water; but a piece of jewelry that lays on our skin every day and ends up in our child's hand—we just don't think about it."[95]

The fact that Hughes *has* thought about it and solved the problem has turned Mommy Necklaces into a global brand. She now has customers across the United States and in New Zealand and Australia (two markets flooded with China imports) and over sixteen thousand Facebook fans. Amazingly, their biggest order for the month of July 2012 came from a retailer in China!

Ironically, as her business ramped up, her US-based bead supplier, Greene Plastics, filed for state receivership in Rhode Island.[96] Greene lost its biggest customer when Walmart decided to drop them as a vendor and begin sourcing their beads from a company that imports them from China.

CHAPTER 7

The Power of We— Building Great Teams

Harmony among people is the basis of the way of military operations.[97]
The Art of War

Sarah and Viktor Lytvinenko shared an urge to start a company that made comfortable, stylish USA-made blue jeans in Raleigh, North Carolina. But with no apparel manufacturing background, their first attempts were, to quote Sarah, "terrible."[98] So they sold an old video camera and a bike, used the proceeds to buy a few industrial sewing machines, and turned for guidance to veterans from the area's closed denim factories to learn the business. A YouTube video clip from 2010 shows that many of the employees in the Lytvinenkos' cut and sew operation at the time were seasoned veterans of the textile business. Those mentors helped them through the start-up phase of a now thriving company, Raleigh Denim.

Perhaps the biggest challenge of implementing the principles of *fewer*, *faster*, and *finer* is changing your company's culture. The old business model of producing long runs with extended lead times does not create the same pressure cooker environment as an operation that produces smaller orders very quickly. Functioning smoothly and effectively in this environment requires a very particular type of employee, and even the most updated automation equipment in the world is no substitute.

By 2008 I was convinced we had a viable business model at Trans-Tex and that business conditions were moving in our favor—that we could not only compete with the China factories, but beat them. However, we would need to change the culture of the company to do so, and we would need a team of people who understood the model, had experienced the daily pressure of satisfying customer demands for small orders delivered quickly, and had the attitude to do what was necessary to exploit the weaknesses of the China factories. At Trans-Tex, the key members of the team that transformed the culture—and drove our success—came from Quill and Just-A-Stretch, two companies decimated by offshoring.

What were the attributes that made them as individuals, and Trans-Tex as a company, successful?

- **Experience**—Gray hair is good. Experienced people, in general, are battle tested and have dealt with both high and low volume levels of business. They can identify ways to reduce minimum order sizes, shorten lead times, and improve quality.
- **Sense of urgency**—Production lead times being so compressed, the loss of one hour—whether in customer service, order entry, production, or shipping—can cost you 5 percent or more of your lead time. Each individual member of your team must move efficiently from task to task and know how to prioritize.
- **Levelheadedness**—They never get too up or too down. They do not get flustered when the workload suddenly doubles. People with this quality can handle the stressful spikes in business that will result from the *fewer, faster,* and *finer* business model.
- **Flexibility**—They have the willingness and capability to wear many hats and to adapt to increased business levels without wilting under pressure. This is a particularly important attribute if your company is small.
- **Willingness to be a team player**—If you have an employee who is willing to quietly help out a coworker to move the ball forward for the team as a whole, you've got a winner.

Fifty is the New Thirty

Dana Floyd was hired as an information services manager straight out of college. She had no experience hiring or firing but was thankful for the opportunity she had been given and determined to succeed. Because her company was ramping up, Dana was compelled to fill a number of data entry positions over the course of a few months. As it would be for most of us, her default position was to hire someone just graduating from college. Having been given the chance to prove herself, she wanted to extend that opportunity to other recent graduates. The result? A staff with too much turnover, attendance problems, bad attitudes, and high levels of personal drama. After several years of constantly training new hires, she decided to take a different tack and consider more mature candidates for those positions. Almost immediately the department stabilized.

"Currently, my team ranges from 23 to 74 years old," Dana says, "so I don't want to sound like I'm bashing all young workers. I have some very bright, hard-working young rock stars that will do amazing things in their careers. However, in my experience they have been hard to find. When I shifted to hiring more experienced personnel I saw immediate results. The new hire training sessions dropped from 6 per year to 1 per year to once every 2 years. Attendance problems are now almost non-existent. Productivity and accuracy increase year over year."[99] Dana discovered the hard way that gray hair is good.

A Trans-Tex customer once had someone call us anonymously to test us as to whether we were selling to, or would consider selling to, their customer. Of course, Trans-Tex would never sell to our customer's customer because it ran counter to our business model, but if the person at our end taking the call had been less experienced, they would not have understood the complexities of our marketplace and might have inadvertently placed us in a delicate position with our customer.

When I first became involved with Trans-Tex and decided to pursue a strategy targeting promotional products suppliers, no one in the Trans-Tex organization understood that network. I knew that if we were to jump into that market with both feet and implement the principles of *fewer, faster,* and *finer,* we would need people on the front lines who understood the players in the distribution network and grasped the threat posed by China manufacturers. We ran an ad that specifically asked for applicants with promotional products experience. The ad was answered by Pat Fontana, whom I had first met twenty-three years previously when we were freshmen at Providence College. She started in the promotional products business in 1985 with ArtMold, a promotional products supplier company based in Providence. She remained with the company until 2003, when the Providence operation was closed and consolidated into one of their parent company's operations in New London, Wisconsin. During her years at ArtMold and Norwood, I would run into Pat occasionally at promotional products trade shows, where she would help staff the company's trade show booth.

After Norwood moved the ArtMold operation to the Midwest, Fontana worked for another promotional products supplier and then an offset printing company. Since Trans-Tex would be expanding more aggressively into the promotional products space, I knew that we needed someone with the aptitude to quickly learn the ropes of the traditional printed webbing business but who also understood the event-driven nature of promotional products orders. Fontana had a clear understanding of the distribution network and the experience to handle the administrative pressure of a ramp-up in sales and order count. She joined Trans-Tex in 2007 and immediately stabilized our customer service and order entry functions.

Two years later, I had the great fortune to hear that Jayne Corrente, with whom I had worked for twenty years at Quill, was available due to the sale of Quill to Newell Rubbermaid. When Jayne was first hired at Quill, the customer service/order entry department was still in the basement level of the tenement house on River Avenue in Providence. At the time, we had only one other person in the department. By the time I left Quill fifteen years later, Jayne was managing a team of twelve. During the interim, she had expertly shepherded the department through dramatic sales increases at the same time that production lead times in the business were shrinking each year. Unflappable, smart, and highly experienced, she was without question both the best customer service person *and* best customer service manager I had ever encountered. It was a quick and easy decision to bring Jayne on board.

One of the key attributes shared by Pat and Jayne is that both had worked for many years with supplier companies like those we were targeting, so they completely understood the mind-set and motivations of our new customer base. There was no need to instruct them on the idiosyncrasies of the marketplace because they had both lived in it for over twenty years.

Pat and Jayne were instrumental in our success at Trans-Tex because, once they learned the details of the dye sublimation printing process, they were ready for the heat of battle and capable of intelligently discussing our products and processes with any of our customers, including those who had been with Trans-Tex for decades. Their experience made them invaluable. If you are focusing your company on the principles of *fewer, faster,* and *finer,* hiring people in leadership positions with solid experience is critical to your success. With subsequent hires, you may have the luxury of bringing in a younger or less experienced person and training him or her, but not for a team leadership position. And if you are a small company that needs only one person on the front line to communicate with customers, lean toward people who have years of industry-specific experience in a fast-paced environment. Never forget that gray hair is good.

In April 2015 I was visiting Quick Fitting in Warwick, Rhode Island, and their lean manufacturing guru, Paul Cary, introduced me to Herb Bouchard. Cary had coaxed Bouchard to come to Quick Fitting to help implement the company's lean initiative. Within a matter of weeks, Bouchard had cut the lead time from new product concept to physical prototype from weeks to days. Only an experienced hand can make such an immediate and dramatic impact.

Don't Just Do Something; Stand There

If you've spent any length of time as part of a team, then you know the type. They shuffle along instead of striding. Their default action when something impedes progress is to do nothing. They wait for the work to come to them instead of seeking out something to do. They table problems instead of raising a red flag. All these are symptoms of someone with no sense of urgency; and a sense of urgency is an essential quality when you are dropping lead times and order size while working to keep quality first-rate.

People with a true sense of urgency are constantly on the move with a spring in their step—not in an officious or boisterous way, but quietly and efficiently. They finish what they start, even when difficult obstacles are encountered. They are generally engaging and bright-eyed. They are friendly and helpful and tend to lift spirits when they enter a room. For this type of person, making a concerted effort, even if it leads to an occasional mistake, is always better than doing nothing. Their default position is taking action. That attitude is a key to implementing the principles of *fewer, faster,* and *finer* in your organization.

Take care not to confuse a person with a genuine sense of urgency with the type of person that I characterize as a "human tornado." Like the meteorological tornado, such people make a lot of noise and sow destruction wherever they erratically land. Their constant fluttering about is meant more to show their coworkers how busy and important they are than it is about trying to get something done. That type of personality is actually destructive to your organization because what they do is driven primarily by ego and not the benefit of the team as a whole. You can tell the difference between a "human tornado" and an employee with a sense of urgency by looking at the result of each moment of truth they have with a team member. Did their encounter spur movement toward a solution to a problem, or was the problem simply exacerbated? Tornados turn small problems into bigger ones. People with a sense of urgency are always moving toward a solution, either alone or in concert with team members.

Several months ago I was interviewing Karl Wadensten, the president of Vibco in Wyoming, Rhode Island, for one of a series of company profiles for the American Dragon video series. During the interview, Karl described the type of individual a company needs to implement lean principles. Not surprisingly, his description also applies to the type of team leader you need to implement the principles of *fewer, faster,* and *finer.* "You need the Braveheart," Wadensten said, "the Mel Gibson cry; you have to have the war paint on." He meant, of course, that you need people with a sense of mission and urgency. This doesn't mean that your best people cannot lead quietly; only that they must lead.

At Trans-Tex, we had dropped production times from weeks to days and, in some cases, to hours. Every hour, indeed, every minute, counts in that type of environment. We were fortunate to have Bob Laferriere as our operations manager during the ramp-up. When we hired him, I harbored some doubts about how he would fit in with our business model. In my experience, second-generation businesspeople tend to play not to lose, instead of playing to win; they often lack a sense of urgency, and that usually leads to slow decision making and even slower execution. But Bob was the exception that proved the rule.

He had a bit of a chip on his shoulder due to the offshoring of the textile business and its effect on his family business Just-A-Stretch. Watching him work, it was apparent that he had been born with a sense of urgency. If you walked out onto the Trans-Tex factory floor, it was rare to see Bob sitting at his desk—and when he was at his desk, it was to check inventory levels and place purchase orders for parts and material.

Finding Bob on the floor was a constant challenge. He might be helping to set up a run on the transfer machines, diagnosing a problem on the huge flexography presses, or laying out a production schedule in assembly. And he moved from department to department so quickly that I was often chasing him from one to the other to catch up to him. Oftentimes I simply resorted to calling him on his cell phone to save myself the trek. This constant, yet effective, movement was illustrative of Bob's ingrained sense of urgency. Bob understood that Trans-Tex could not be a *faster* company unless he was *faster*.

On an Even Keel

At one point during the Trans-Tex ramp-up, the number of lanyard orders was so high and so constant that the lead times on some of our industrial business began to backslide. Until we righted the ship on that front, we had a few very unhappy customers for about six weeks. We were fortunate that we had Fran Anderson as our frontline person to manage our industrial accounts through the rough patch. Fran had spent twenty-nine years with a local four-color printer. Because Trans-Tex specialized in dye sublimation printing, Fran's skills and knowledge base were highly transferable to her position working with Trans-Tex's industrial customers.

Aside from her experience level, Fran possessed an invaluable skill—she was levelheaded, never getting too up or too down. This is an important skill no matter one's place in an organization, but it is particularly important in the customer service area. During a ramp-up engendered by implementation of the *fewer, faster,* and *finer* model, production stresses will inevitably occur. Keeping a level head as the amount of stress rises will reassure customers and team members. Fran did her best to keep distraught customers informed, worked closely with operations manager Bob Laferriere to prioritize the workflow, and never cracked. Unless you've been on the front lines, it's difficult to understand how stressful it can be to take call after call from unhappy customers and still keep them on your company's side. Fran managed it coolly and professionally.

This attribute is not only important on the front lines, however. Team leaders in production stress points must also stay even-keeled to prevent a department from spinning out of control. Because we custom printed our products, every order at Trans-Tex had to flow through our graphics department. Keep in mind that the company went from processing several orders a month to hundreds of orders a month. Each of those orders had artwork that needed to be manipulated and printed to fit onto the narrow webbing—and it had to be done within the space of a few hours. Michael Whitt was sitting in the belly of that beast.

Whitt had run the graphic art department at Quill during their growth in the late '80s and the '90s, so he knew the stress of a ramp-up. But what had happened at Quill was not as dramatic as the growth at Trans-Tex. At one point, over a six-month period, the number of orders increased so dramatically that there simply wasn't enough machine time on the digital presses to accommodate the growth. During that spurt we replaced slower digital presses with faster ones, but still it wasn't enough to keep up—so we bought even more of the faster digital printers. And for each order that needed to be printed on the digital press, there was a piece of artwork that needed to be manipulated. During that period, Mike quietly raised the alarm about the lack of machine capacity but then put his head down and worked to handle the surge. It was a rocky journey for a few weeks, but Mike's calm demeanor and work ethic kept the boat afloat.

I vividly remember meeting Vibco's production manager, John Goodwin, during my tour of their plant. He appears in Vibco's American Dragon webisode, discussing how reducing setup time allows an operation to not only move *faster,* but also produce smaller orders more cost-effectively. A lean manufacturing operation like Vibco, by its very nature, must execute quickly. But as impressed as I was with the speed and smoothness of their operation, I was similarly impressed by Goodwin's almost preternatural calm. People like Goodwin, Mike Whitt, and Fran Anderson are efficient yet calming influences when all hell breaks loose in a manufacturing operation.

The importance of having experienced team leaders to implement the principles of *fewer*, *faster*, and *finer* was noted earlier. It's no surprise that experienced people are typically the most levelheaded because they've been through storms and learned how to weather them. However, those attributes are not inextricably linked. If you have the opportunity to bring on board a younger person with little experience but who appears levelheaded and demonstrates a sense of urgency, make the hire.

Bend, Don't Break

Love them or hate them, no one can deny that the New England Patriots are one of the most successful sports franchises of the last fifteen years. One of the key reasons is their business model. They don't just draft and trade for the best available athlete based on the standard measurements for speed, strength, or jumping ability. They look for players that are the best fit for their system. And that system requires most players to have a high degree of adaptability. Want to have a chance to stick with the Patriots? Make sure you do your job on a particular play, but also demonstrate the ability to play multiple positions.

When I first became involved with Trans-Tex, the production equipment was generally in a state of disrepair, and there was no one on staff who had the expertise to maintain it, much less fix it when it broke down. This can be challenging enough when you are fulfilling a relatively small number of orders with long production runs and no established delivery date. However, at Trans-Tex we were slashing minimum order sizes and drastically reducing lead times, while coping with a huge increase in order count. In that type of atmosphere, especially if you run a relatively small operation, one idle machine can cripple your operation. We needed a MacGyver type who could fix most anything and keep it running smoothly.

Fortunately, Paul Corrente, another former Quill employee, was available. Having seen his work at Quill, I knew that Paul had the talent to keep the machines running. But he was also extremely versatile; while at Quill he had spent time in general plant maintenance, had worked in the tool room, and had even spent a little time in product development. His versatility made Paul a very valuable addition to our team during the ramp-up. He not only kept the machines running; he also functioned as a de facto second-in-command to Bob Laferriere. When necessary, Paul would even jump into a production position to keep the work flowing through the factory. He also had a wry sense of humor that lightened the mood when the going got tough. But it was his flexibility, his willingness to wear a number of different hats, that made him so vital to our success.

When key employees have both a versatile skill set and the willingness to use those skills in whatever manner possible to benefit the team effort, a company can climb any mountain.

Put Me In, Coach

It is apparent that teamwork is important to any manufacturing operation, particularly one that is implementing the principles of *fewer, faster,* and *finer*. However, some team players are born, and some are made. In my experience, the best are born. You'll know them because they don't work with one eye on the time clock. If they see that a colleague needs help, they pitch in. When extra hours are needed to finish a particularly important job, they always show up. We had several at Trans-Tex, but two are particularly good examples.

When I first began working with Trans-Tex, Matilde Beltre seemed simply one of several women in assembly who, not being terribly busy at the time, would occasionally pop open a book to read while waiting for the next order to arrive. However, as the business ramped up, she proved to be far more talented than I had initially recognized.

As the assembly staff grew from four to over twenty people, Beltre seemed to easily integrate new people, while maintaining consistent order flow. She and most of her assembly staff spoke Spanish as their first language, and Matilde was one of the few fluent in English. But for Matilde, language was no barrier to productivity. Keep in mind that the lanyard assembly process was not automated, so the only way to scale up the department was to add personnel. During our ramp-up stage, the assembly team could always be counted on to finish the jobs on time and work any extra hours—on any day of the week—to ensure that orders were ready on time. Since most of the lanyard orders were for specific events, being one day late was considered failure: if we did not have the product to the customer on or before the day of the event, the lanyards would no longer be needed. But Matilde and her team were always up to the task. The very few times that we did miss an in-hands date (I can count them on one hand), it was not for lack of effort.

On my strolls through her department, it was always quiet and orderly, even as the head count quadrupled. At times she was constrained for space, but Matilde never seemed to get flustered, always managed to accurately prioritize the orders queued up for assembly, and kept her team focused on the task at hand. She also worked amicably with team leaders in other departments. This is a critical skill when the pressure of much higher order counts and quicker turn times can create interdepartmental conflict. Matilde proved to be both an effective team leader *and* team player.

Tino De Carvalho, like Matilde Beltre, was employed at Trans-Tex when I first became involved. Tino was a rock in the transfer department. The type of work he was asked to do changed quite a bit during our ramp-up, but Tino took on all new tasks without missing a beat. He consistently produced high-quality work and was extremely reliable, almost never missing a day. Perhaps because he had little confidence in his English-speaking ability, Tino always seemed very quiet. What I didn't realize was that he was quietly figuring out how to run the department.

In 2015 we experienced a record first quarter, with business up over 27 percent. This created stress across all departments, but particularly in the transfer area, where we had survived for years without a nominal team leader. Bob Laferriere asked Tino to step up and fill that role, and he did so without hesitation. Tino had garnered a great deal of respect from his coworkers because of his knowledge and work habits, so they immediately accepted Tino as their team leader, and the department's performance just as quickly improved. He taught me that a quiet, steady leader can have a greater sense of urgency and attention to detail than the "human tornado," who creates a whirl of activity but little in the way of results.

Of course, there are many people who make a great operation tick, and these are only a few of the people who were instrumental in the ramp-up at Trans-Tex. But the people I mentioned above displayed particular characteristics or attitudes that can transform the culture of a company and enable it to handle the increased stresses that the *fewer, faster,* and *finer* business model creates. This allows one to manage by exception instead of micromanaging every detail of the organization, allowing upper management to focus on more strategic matters. When you have colleagues with the above attributes and they approach you with a problem, your first response should always be, "What do you recommend?" You'll find that 95 percent of the time, they have the right answer.

Thanks, But No Thanks

Just as there are people particularly suited to implementing *fewer, faster,* and *finer,* there are those who will not thrive in that environment. We went through our share at Trans-Tex and could tell very quickly if someone would not be a good fit. In general, these are some attitudes and characteristics that should give one pause:

- **Youth**

    I realize this will sound harsh and that I seem like an old codger, and this won't garner me a lot of fans among the younger generation. However, in most instances, youth is the flip side of experience. Young people tend to be less focused on the job at hand. They are often impatient and anxious about moving on to the next thing (or the next job). If success (however one defines it) doesn't happen quickly, they often don't have the drive to fight through it. However, find a patient young person with willingness to learn and persevere, and you've got a winner. As noted above, they are a great second hire in a small company. But go with experience first.

- **Stuck in a Rut**

    This is the biggest downside to focusing on experience when hiring. Be wary of bringing onboard an experienced person who seems to be stuck in a rut. Usually such people come from larger companies that service stable and mature markets. They think the only solution to a problem is the one that has worked for them for the past twenty years. But in a ramp-up spurred by the implementation of *fewer, faster,* and *finer,* what people did in their prior job and how they did it may not apply.

    At Trans-Tex we went through a number of experienced shippers before finally finding one who could handle the stress and strains of our business model. Due to our quick turnaround times, many packages landed in the shipping department mere minutes before the UPS or FedEx truck would arrive for pickup. This tsunami of packages at the last minute is not typical in most manufacturing companies, so new ways needed to be devised to accommodate this daily rush. A shipper accustomed to either a small number of shipments or a large number of shipments spaced evenly throughout the day had a lot of adjustments to make. We averaged one shipper per year until we found an experienced person who both knew how to ship and could handle the strain. If you can't find an experienced shipper who can make it in this environment, hire someone with a great attitude and teach him or her to ship. Attitude is more important than the skill set.

- **Outsized Ego**

    Earlier in the chapter I described the human tornado who makes a lot of noise and accomplishes little. Then there is "the specialist," who believes that he or she was hired for a particular job. When things become hectic, this person refuses to help out because he or she thinks his or her job level is too important to be performing what he or she considers menial tasks. And finally we have the "pontificator," who has plenty of time to tell everyone else how to do their job, but doesn't do his or her own job very well. All of the above are character types who suboptimize the team for their own agenda, and they are anathema to the *fewer, faster,* and *finer* business model. They are an expensive distraction in an operation handling a lot of small, customized orders at dizzying speeds.

- **Family**

    Even though they may be a good fit for a particular position, hiring family members for a *fewer, faster,* and *finer* ramp-up has many more potential downsides than upsides. It's unfair, but unless the family member works harder than everyone else, he or she will likely be branded a slacker. When the inevitable crunch time comes, if family members slip up even once, the finger-pointing or the whispering campaign will begin. In many instances, it simply puts the family member under too much pressure. Avoid hiring family members if you can.

Bouncing Back

Darius Mir offshored production for his business, 9to5 Seating, to China in the early 2000s. As the decade wore on, Mir became frustrated by the increasing costs in China and the resulting challenge of finding and keeping skilled workers. After doing some research, Mir realized that, using automation, he could get the same productivity from five US workers that he got from twenty-two workers in China. So he reshored production to Tennessee, where he employs forty people with hopes of doubling that within a few months. The average wage for unskilled production workers will be eleven dollars an hour.[100]

Clearly, this is a lower wage rate, adjusted for inflation, than was prevalent in most unionized factories in the 1970s. The wave of offshoring that occurred over the last thirty-five years has, unfortunately, put heavy downward pressure on wages in the manufacturing sector. During the trough of the Great Recession, talented and experienced people were out of work for months. Many have been hired back at wage levels below what they were making ten years ago. If you are a manufacturer and your business is ramping up, why not hire them back at the wage levels they previously had? Isn't hiring them at levels below what they earned ten or fifteen years ago taking advantage of good people?

We must keep in mind that even though the disadvantages of importing are increasing, it remains necessary for US manufacturers struggling against overseas competition to keep their selling prices within shouting range of that competition. This is a sad fact of life that individual manufacturing companies cannot change, and they will respond by hiring at prevailing wage rates. As we slowly win the battle against the imports, pressure on wages will eventually turn upward, and manufacturing workers will begin to gain ground on the wage front. It will be an incremental process. Let's get the jobs back first, even though they may pay less than they once did. Then, as companies begin to win battles against overseas competition, the wage levels will begin to rise. But first we must win battles, one order at a time.

As important as it is to remain as competitive as possible with wage rates, it is just as critical to maintain a willingness to pay higher wages to quality people. When we started down the *fewer, faster,* and *finer* path at Trans-Tex, we had some employees in key positions that clearly did not possess the skills necessary to implement our strategy, and our mediocre performance reflected that. As we upgraded the quality and pay of people in those positions, we operated more quickly and efficiently, and the higher wage rates were more than justified by the improved company performance.

People Power

At Trans-Tex, the final piece of the personnel puzzle was the owners, Phil Barr and Skip Hebert. Unlike many business owners that I had encountered in the past, they steadfastly believed in the *fewer, faster,* and *finer* business model and continued to invest in our success. This was difficult at first, as we needed to significantly increase costs initially to upgrade people and equipment to handle both the sudden influx of business and the much shorter production lead times. But they determinedly stayed the course.

However, the most important "people" story was that we never could have handled the increase in our order count and the required speed to market without hiring some of the best, most experienced people who had once worked for companies like Quill and Just-A-Stretch, both of which had succumbed to the globalization of their respective industries and the outsourcing of their jobs to other states or other countries.

I was visiting Trans-Tex recently, and while sitting in the conference room, I heard a loud cheer coming from the production floor. Curious about what caused the ruckus, I walked out to the factory and ran into the office manager distributing the weekly paychecks. When I asked her about the cheers, she smiled and said, "Oh, that's just the people in the assembly department. They're always so happy when they get their check." Now, keep in mind that these are not highly paid people. They perform hand assembly work in a basic manufacturing industry. And, no, these cheers weren't a calculated sarcastic outburst of mock joy. It was a demonstration of simple enthusiasm from a team of people happy to be paid for a job well done and happy that their products are "Made in the U.S.A."

People, not machines, are the key to success in any manufacturing operation, whether advanced or basic. This is sometimes forgotten in the emphasis on advanced manufacturing and automation. Not that this emphasis is a bad thing; on the contrary, it is essential to the United States remaining in the manufacturing vanguard. However, as that laudable transition to advanced manufacturing rolls along, we must not throw basic manufacturing under the bus. Basic manufacturers often become advanced manufacturers over the course of time through the combination of hard work and smart investment. And those hand assembly jobs can eventually become machine-tending jobs that pay much more.

In discussing manufacturing jobs in basic industries, pundits often question whether we as a country really want these jobs. Largely because of the pay scale, many consider them an anachronism. Local and national economic development efforts focus almost exclusively on advanced manufacturing, be it technology, biomed, or the next big thing. But after hearing those workers cheer, whenever someone asks me whether we want those jobs, I ask them, "Who is this 'we' you're talking about?" Perhaps professors of economics sitting in faculty lounges on bucolic college campuses don't want those jobs, and perhaps financial analysts at think tanks don't want those jobs; but there are millions of unemployed or underemployed Americans who do. And thousands of small to midsize manufacturers who want to provide those jobs. Give me an army of people like that group at Trans-Tex, and I'll rule the manufacturing world.

On any great team, the players need to be a good fit for the system. The *fewer, faster*, and *finer* business model, due to its constraints and pressures, is most effective when executed by people with the following traits and characteristics:

- experience
- sense of urgency
- levelheadedness
- flexibility
- willingness to be a team player

If you can find employees that fit this description, hire them—even if they are not trained in a particular skill. Remember that skills can be taught, but attitude cannot.

CHAPTER 8

A Small Price to Pay—The Role of the Consumer and B2B Buyer

Adaptation means not clinging to fixed methods, but changing appropriately according to events, acting as is suitable.[101]
The Art of War

In 2012 Bruce Cochrane, the president of Lincolnton Furniture, was the guest of the first lady at Barack Obama's State of the Union address. Cochrane's family had been in the furniture manufacturing business in North Carolina for three generations. The family had sold their business in 1996 because they felt they could no longer compete with low-cost Asian imports. The buyer of their business eventually moved production to China, and 1,300 US manufacturing jobs were lost. By then, Bruce Cochrane had become a consultant for companies that offshored production to Asia.

While working in China, he noticed a demand there for US-made goods and decided to resume production in the United States under the Lincolnton brand. He hired sixty people, many of whom had previously worked for the family, and reopened the plant. Glowing local news coverage followed, and the story went national. Cochrane found himself in Washington, DC, at Obama's Insourcing Jobs Forum, where he was hailed by the president as the leader of a company "choosing to invest in the one country with the most productive workers, the best universities, and the most creative and innovative entrepreneurs in the world, and that is the United States of America." Later that week Cochrane sat next to Michelle Obama at the State of the Union address.

One year later, Lincolnton Furniture quietly closed its doors. At the time, Bruce Cochrane did not return Associated Press calls asking for comments. Company CFO Ben Causey said the company folded due to lack of orders.[102]

Depending on the consumer to pay more for US-made products strictly out of patriotism has proven to be a business model with short legs. Manufacturing long runs of commodity products in the same manner you always have and then simply slapping a "Made in the U.S.A." label on the box as a marketing panacea is a prescription for failure. As manufacturers, if we are going to compete aggressively with overseas competition, we must provide products and service in a manner that our competitors cannot match, using the principles of *fewer, faster,* and *finer*. The product should be shorn of as much commoditization as possible, offer customization options, be delivered exactly where and when the customer wants it, and have a clear quality advantage over the imports. If you are making the same thing that a China manufacturer makes, delivering it in the same slow manner, selling it at a higher price than the import and relying on your Made in the U.S.A. pedigree to win the day, you are whistling past the graveyard.

That being said, consumers and B2B buyers can play a role in the effort to reshore US manufacturing jobs—and that doesn't mean paying more for a product simply because it's made in the United States of America. As consumers and B2B buyers, we must change our definition of smart shopping. For most of us, smart shopping means comparing products that appear to be similar and buying the one with the lowest price. But that's not being smart; that's being a sucker, because the product with the lowest price may not be the product with the lowest total cost.

Kicking the Habit—The Role of B2B Buyers

Harry Moser was frustrated. He had spent his entire career in domestic manufacturing, including over four decades selling machine tools and foundry equipment. He had anxiously watched the slow, steady stream of offshored US manufacturing jobs become a tsunami as the new millennium dawned and decided he'd seen enough of it. In the mid-2000s, as president and then chairman of +GF+ Machining Solutions, Moser lobbied the Association for Manufacturing Technology, the National Tooling and Machining Association, and the Precision Metalforming Association to join forces to support reshoring efforts that would ensure the future sales and use of US-made machine tools.

Transitioning out of his role with +GF+, he began making presentations and writing articles on how to beat Chinese competition in the US market. Having read the canon on the hidden costs of importing, he noted that almost every writer mentioned the costs that many procurement departments ignore when comparing the price of an imported part to a domestically made part and that they all stressed that buyers should make purchasing decisions based on what is called the "total cost of ownership." However, not one writer offered a spreadsheet that would allow a purchasing manager to actually calculate that total cost. It was surprising to Moser that a profession that so values accurate numbers did not have a simple tool to accurately calculate the true cost of ownership so that a comparison could be made between the cost of buying or making an import vs. the cost of buying or making a domestic part. He decided to change that.

In 2010 Moser founded the Reshoring Initiative with a mission of bringing good, well-paying manufacturing jobs back to the United States by assisting companies to more accurately assess their total cost of offshoring and shift collective thinking from "offshoring is cheaper" to "domestic reduces the total cost of ownership." Job One for Moser was to delve back into all the articles he had read and list the myriad costs, risks, and strategic impacts that affect total cost of ownership. He then wrote software that would assign dollar values to each item on the list and had the software critiqued by colleagues from across the country, most notably by his contacts at the Association for Manufacturing Excellence. That software became the Total Cost of Ownership Estimator, which now resides on the Reshoring Initiative website and can be used at no charge by any purchasing department interested in calculating the true cost of importing. Since the site was launched, the estimator has been used over 1,500 times.

The Total Cost of Ownership Estimator is an excellent tool to help one better understand the difference between the price of something and its total cost. The *price* of an item is the amount of money that exchanges hands for the item. It's simple. The price of the widget is $2.00, so I give the cashier $2.00. The total *cost* of an item is fully loaded with other factors that determine whether the purchase is actually a good value.

For B2B buyers, this comparison can be particularly critical. In determining the total cost of ownership, B2B buyers must weigh not only the price of a widget, but also such factors as:

- the minimum order size. (If you are forced to order a higher amount, then negative cash cycle ramifications must be added into the total cost.)
- the length of time until delivery. (If it takes a long time before you receive the product, then you need to order higher amounts—which costs more—to prevent an out-of-stock situation.)
- ease of communication with the source. (If poor communication issues due to either time zone differences or language problems cause your employees to constantly call or e-mail the vendor, the additional cost of the employee's time must also be considered.)
- poor quality. (If you reject parts and/or replace defective product made from those parts, then the cost of this waste must also be added in to arrive at the total cost.)
- supply chain disruption risk (e.g., political instability in the overseas manufacturer's country or strikes at shipping ports).

As the pricing gap narrows between imports and domestically made products and parts, calculating the total cost of ownership becomes ever more critical. Even the Commerce Department has recognized the importance of the total cost of ownership approach to measuring the speed and effectiveness of supply chain partners. Their March 2015 report titled "Supply Chain Innovation: Strengthening America's Small Manufacturers" notes that when a manufacturer uses a total cost of ownership approach to sourcing—instead of simply buying from the supplier with the lowest per piece cost—the additional costs of added shipping time, risk of inventory being damaged during transport, and interruptions of the supply chain become more readily apparent.[103]

B2B buyers can play a role in the renaissance of US manufacturing by simply breaking the habit of automatically buying from overseas and redoing the math on whether importing parts—or moving manufacturing overseas—is the cost-effective investment decision. US manufacturers of B2B parts don't want handouts; they simply want a level playing field. By taking a close look at the total cost instead of the price per piece, US B2B buyers can level that playing field.

Of course, the TCO Estimator is only helpful if you have a domestic part to compare against an import. And if you are a B2B buyer accustomed to simply reordering the same part from the same overseas vendor, how do you find US manufacturers for that part? You turn to a company that was protecting domestic supply chains before their survival was even an issue.

Nurturing Domestic B2B Supply Chains

Ben Edwards and his wife, Marge, are pioneers in the efforts to reshore US manufacturing. But they started so long ago that, at the time, they couldn't possibly understand the long-term importance of what they created. Ben is a former marine who began his manufacturing career selling the services of a custom metal stamping job shop in Waterbury, Connecticut, throughout the Northeast during the late '60s and early '70s. During his sales calls, Ben would constantly bang heads with purchasing agents looking for not only the lowest price, but for supply chain partners "that we can come and talk to."

He sensed an opportunity. What if he could bring together small to midsize domestic parts providers and introduce them to manufacturers, creating a network of relationships on a regional or national basis instead of a merely local basis? This would provide the original equipment manufacturers (OEMs) with a broader range of US-sourcing options, while giving parts providers access to potential buyers throughout the country. Thus, if their home region was economically depressed, they might still survive by developing OEM accounts in other regions of the country.

Thus was born the Job Shop Company. Ben and Marge mortgaged their house in Prospect, Connecticut, and began producing trade shows under the name "The Job Shop Capabilities and Custom Components Show." It took them ten years to establish four shows held yearly in different regions of the country. As their trade shows slowly took hold, the offshoring craze was decimating US domestic manufacturing. OEMs were either moving production offshore or shutting down production altogether and becoming importers of finished product. Meanwhile, the small job shops that relied on those once-domestic manufacturers were finding it increasingly difficult to survive. As those smaller companies succumbed to the waves of offshoring, US manufacturing supply chains began to disappear. What held the remaining supply chains together during these dark days? Ben's company.

Eventually the offshoring pendulum began to swing back as costs in China began to rise. By 2007 Ben had changed the name of the trade show to "Design-2-Part." He eventually expanded the number of show offerings to eleven, in locations ranging from Long Beach, California, to Marlborough, Massachusetts. In addition to the trade shows, the company created a website that includes a searchable database of US parts manufacturers. Need a particular type of custom part or service? Simply go to the company's supplier directory[104], type in the service you need and the region of the country from which you hope to buy, and get a list of companies that can build your part. This database is a comprehensive resource featuring nearly two thousand of the finest providers of custom parts, prototypes, components, and design services in North America.

To further enhance the community of US job shop manufacturers, *Design-2-Part Magazine* has been launched. The magazine features articles that help OEMs find solutions to tough manufacturing problems with cutting-edge information and education. By publicizing the accomplishments and manufacturing capabilities of contract manufacturers, *Design-2-Part Magazine* makes it easy for OEMs and product manufacturers to find the resources they need to build higher-quality products. Readers include design engineers, manufacturing engineers, manufacturing managers, and purchasing managers employed by OEMs and makers of finished products.

The Job Shop Company held together the domestic supply chain of small US job shops when offshoring decimated US manufacturing, and they are here now as smart B2B buyers begin to look at the total cost of ownership. Stuck in a rut ordering imported parts because you think there is no US-made alternative? Check out Design-2-Part, identify a US manufacturer for the part you need, and then use the TCO Estimator to determine whether the imported product truly costs less than the domestic product.

New Blood—The Role of Entrepreneurs

Matthew Burnett had manufacturing in his blood. His father moved their family to Detroit for a job with Ford while Matthew was still a youngster. He grew up hearing manufacturing stories at the dinner table. And during his teenage years, he watched a city that was once the most important manufacturing hub in the United States fall slowly into decay.

After four years studying industrial engineering in college, Matthew was designing watches for major brands such as Marc Jacobs and DKNY, and he saw the manufacturing of those designs offshored to other countries. Born with an entrepreneurial spirit, he eventually decided to begin designing and sourcing his own brand of watches. Not surprisingly, he quickly discovered that the hurdles of overseas production for a start-up were far more daunting than for a major brand. Minimum order sizes were so high and production lead times so extended that he would be forced to bring in far more product than he could afford. He knew the solution was domestic sourcing, but where would he find the manufacturers he needed? Did a domestic supply chain for watches even exist?

Eventually Matthew was able to construct a domestic supply chain that allowed him to produce in two weeks what would take three months overseas. During that process the idea of a potentially disruptive business model emerged. Why not create a website for product entrepreneurs that would make their prospective US supply chain transparent *and* speed up the product development process? He knew that over 75 percent of first-time entrepreneurs fail to get their product to the prototype stage. What if he could significantly lower that percentage while supporting US manufacturing jobs?

His solution was Makers Row. Makers Row is essentially a transparent online supply chain solution for entrepreneurs who have never manufactured a product and have no knowledge of the supply chain that their product requires. The Makers Row website breaks down the new product creation process into six easily understandable steps:

1. *Ideation*—taking your product idea to factories that can help you refine it and make it more production-ready.
2. *Pattern making*—pairing you with people who can make blueprints of your product idea.
3. *Material suppliers*—locating companies that manufacture the raw material you need.
4. *Sample makers*—companies that will make the first product prototypes.
5. *Tooling*—manufacturers that create the tooling needed to accelerate production.
6. *Production*—the factories that will actually produce your ultimate design.

US manufacturers that provide these services register with Makers Row and are listed on the website under their appropriate category (or categories). The site now holds the contact information of over 3,400 factories.

Of course, this type of transparency, driven by the Internet, is a threat to those who make money by keeping supply chains hidden and then selling access to them. In a memorable segment of *Small Empires* (episode 8), Matthew and Makers Row cofounder Tanya Menendez recount how they were once threatened by a supply chain consultant who boasted that he knew people that could have them shutdown if he was not included in the Makers Row family.[105] In my experience, a veiled threat is not the best strategy for a job interview.

In June 2015, at a White House panel during the National Week of Making, Matthew neatly encapsulated the company mission when he noted that "We're all about helping the little guy to be able to produce their first company in scale. Streamlined manufacturing should be like making a pizza." Makers Row has enabled the success of entrepreneurs—particularly first-timers—by constructing a transparent online domestic supply chain that allows them to produce *fewer* and to do it *faster*.

The Role of Consumers—Read the Label

One of the first and most important steps any consumer can take before a purchase is to determine the country of origin for a product before making the purchase. Consumers, particularly in the United States, have become lax about noting country of origin of a potential purchase, and by doing so, we have inadvertently enabled the abuse of some overseas workers. It is well known that some countries use prison labor, child labor, and even slave labor for manufacturing and agricultural production. The Bureau of International Labor Affairs, under the aegis of the US Department of Labor, keeps an updated list of products by country that are produced by some manufacturers using child and/or forced labor.[106] Keep in mind that this list is not compiled by a far left organization with a radical agenda; it's compiled by a division of the Department of Labor.

You might be surprised by what you find on the list. For example, if you buy footwear or garments from Bangladesh, the shoes or garment may have been produced using child labor. If you buy rice from Burma, it may have been harvested using child or forced labor. The electronics or toys you buy from China? Could be assembled by either a child or forced labor. If that shirt you just bought for your child was made in Vietnam, it might have been produced by either child or forced labor—or both. Consumers should stay informed of the countries that abuse children and other workers to manufacture goods and stop rewarding them for such activity by not buying their product regardless of the cost savings. But to make that decision, one must begin by identifying the country of origin on either the product's packaging or a label on the product itself.

Let's say you have a preference—and are willing to pay a premium—for a product that's made in the United States of America. What should you look for on the label to be certain you're making the right decision? The Federal Trade Commission has required that if a product is labeled "Made in U.S.A.," then "all or virtually all" of that product must be made domestically. "All or virtually all," according to the FTC website, means that "all significant parts and processing that go into a product must be of U.S. origin." That is, the product should contain no—or negligible—foreign content, and it must be assembled in the United States or one of its territories. Not a lot of wriggle room here.

If a product is assembled in the United States of America but not all of the product parts are domestic, the label or carton marking should read, "Assembled in the U.S. from domestic and imported parts." The FTC does not provide a clear percentage measurement of what "virtually all" means in its definition, but any manufacturer should err on the side of caution when it comes to using the Made in U.S.A. marking.

If you see a label or carton marking that reads "Made in America," does that mean the product is made in the United States of America? Not necessarily. For labeling purposes, the term "America" does not refer to the United States particularly, but includes NAFTA signatories Mexico and Canada. Of course, if you see an American flag marking on a product, don't be fooled. It's meaningless unless you also see a "Made in U.S.A." marking.

None of this prevents unscrupulous manufacturers or counterfeiters from placing "Made in the U.S.A." labels on products made overseas. Even big-box retailers have been caught mislabeling products. In late June 2015, the *New York Post* reported that Walmart had been selling products online labeled as "Made in the U.S.A." that were not. The not-for-profit Truth in Advertising studied the Walmart website and found one hundred items falsely labeled "Made in the U.S.A." Walmart's response? They took down all such labeling on their website. A Walmart spokesperson blamed "internet search engines that won't return an item with a badge in search results."[107]

If you want to be absolutely certain that you are buying consumer goods that were manufactured in the United States, begin by finding a trustworthy online source. Although the Internet helped facilitate the offshoring craze, it has also allowed proponents of US manufacturing to aggregate hundreds of thousands of US-made products and create robust online transactional communities.

Michael McKeldon Woody

Online Consumer Revolution

Todd Lipscomb was holding his baby daughter Lyndsey in his arms for the very first time. He had been on the fast track for several years with a technology company, spending a lot of time on the road, including two stints totaling seven years living in Asia. He had recently been promoted by the company to oversee worldwide operating expenditures totaling over $700 million on a yearly basis. But as he held his newborn daughter in his arms, he was haunted by what he had seen in Asia—legions of people earning low wages working in substandard factories and making products bound for US shores. Meanwhile, millions of US manufacturing workers had been thrown out of jobs and were unemployed or underemployed.

And he began to wonder. Would his daughter know of the greatness of the United States? Would she see our country as a bounty of unlimited opportunity? Would her life as an adult be better than his own?

After days of painful soul-searching, Todd decided that he had to take meaningful action. He resigned from his comfortable position with the technology giant and set his sights on helping to revive the US manufacturing base. But how? Having spent years with a technology company, he fully understood the power of the Internet to create a critical mass of people who believed as he did in the importance of US manufacturing. So, despite having no experience as an Internet entrepreneur, Todd took a leap of faith and made a significant personal investment of both time and treasure to found Made In USA Forever, www.madeinusaforever.com. His goal was to create an information resource and clearinghouse for consumer products manufactured in the United States of America.

Todd knew his way around a balance sheet, but he also realized that if he was going to be successful ramping up his warehouse and website, he would need to create a media campaign that involved print, radio, TV, and online. Although he had no experience dealing with the press, he knew that he would need to learn how to attract and give an effective interview. He was more than comfortable speaking to a roomful of colleagues; addressing an audience of thousands on a national radio show was a totally new environment for him. But as do most people who pursue a dream relentlessly, Todd jumped into the deep end of the pool and decided to learn by doing.

Today his website is visited by millions and features over seven hundred suppliers, with hundreds of thousands of consumer products from apparel to food to tools. To promote the site, Todd has given over three hundred radio interviews, appeared on multiple television programs, and written a book, *Re-made in the USA*. The book tells Todd's story in detail and makes a strong case for the importance of US manufacturing. His regular e-blasts feature deals passed along from his US suppliers to his customers. Even their Facebook page, with over 100,000 friends, has evolved into a potent lobbying force on domestic manufacturing issues.

Go on any website of the large "bricks and clicks" consumer stores or multinational brands and try to figure out whether a particular product is made in the United States of America. Occasionally, the website may mention if a particular product is manufactured here, but for the most part, there is no country of origin labeling on product descriptions for most websites—and the photo of the product almost never reveals the label. One of the major benefits of Todd's site is that you can buy with confidence that everything on madeinusaforever.com is made in the United States of America from made-in-U.S.A. materials.

When I asked Todd about the effect of his website on his domestic suppliers, he was rightfully proud of the exposure he had provided them. "Whereas most retailers treat their suppliers like adversaries," Todd says, "we are truly in the corner of Made in U.S.A. suppliers!" During my efforts to write this book, it has been both educational and gratifying to meet people like Todd who have taken a risk to help US manufacturers. This country needs more like him, because over the course of the last thirty-five years, small to midsize manufacturers have gotten little to no help from their local, state, and especially, federal governments.

CHAPTER 9

The Power to Persevere—Government Must Lead, Follow or Get Out of the Way

The strength or weakness of a country depends upon its generals.[108]
The Art of War

In August 2011 Missouri's Department of Economic Development announced a "Made in Missouri" jobs program. According to a news release from Governor Jay Nixon's office, one of the program's principal aims was "to create thousands of jobs to put Missourians back to work." To launch the program, the department planned to hand out to attendees at the Missouri State Fair six thousand key tags that also held a miniflashlight and a pen. On one side of the key tag was printed the website for the initiative: "jobs.mo.gov." On the other side of the key tag was the sticker "Made in China." On the morning of August 1, a group of volunteers and state employees gathered in the conference room of the agency's director to remove the stickers before the pieces were distributed. The program certainly created a few jobs that morning.[109]

Sad to say, but the above story is not all that unusual. In spite of a great deal of lip service from politicians on both sides of the aisle, government has not been a friend to US manufacturers, particularly over the course of the past twenty-five years. In fact, my advice to manufacturers is to not rely on federal, state, or local government for any help at all. Implement the principles of *fewer, faster,* and *finer* in order to better compete with overseas competition and simply pray that government does nothing to harm you. That being said, I do think that there are eight specific actions that government should take to help level a playing field that is often wildly tilted in favor of our manufacturing competitors based in other countries.

1. Stop Making Bad Trade Deals.

Most of the damage done by the federal government has been through the implementation of unbalanced trade deals. Keep in mind that this is coming from someone who was at one time an ardent free trader and even testified before a US Senate subcommittee in support of NAFTA, declaring that it had not gone far enough. Why my turnaround? To quote the economist Paul Samuelson, "Well, when events change, I change my mind. What would you do?"

We enter into trade agreements under the presumption that they will lead to higher exports and lower-priced goods for US consumers, a virtuous cycle that will be a boon for our economy. In 1995 I believed this to be true. Yet today, the value of our exports is dwarfed by the tide of imported goods, and our trade deficit continues to worsen. Since we granted China Permanent Normalized Trade Relations Status (PNTR) at the turn of the new millennium, unleashing a veritable flood of low-cost imports, median household income has actually *dropped* in the United States, from $57,724 in 2000 to $53,657 in 2014, according to statistics compiled by the Federal Reserve Bank of St. Louis. In fact, since China was granted PNTR, median household income has never been higher than in 1999 (the next highest since then was $57,357 in 2007).[110]

From 2000 until 2007, our total trade deficit soared from $372 billion to $761 billion. Even now, our trade deficit is 36 percent higher than it was in 2000. Meanwhile, our trade deficit with China has skyrocketed. In 1999, the year prior to the United States granting China PNTR, our trade deficit with China was $67 billion. By 2007 it was $259 billion. For 2014, it was a record $343 billion.

Why is this happening? Because we are entering into trade agreements with parties that don't play by the same rules. If I own a factory that manufactures a widget and I'm held to certain wage, safety, and environmental standards, but my overseas competition is held to minimal standards or no standards at all, then my competitor's widget will cost much less than mine. This is simple common sense. Those who disagree will claim that this is a naïve position and that the issue is far more complicated. But it isn't. And I might even reconsider my position if the lower-priced goods coming from overseas meant a better lifestyle for me and my fellow citizens. But our standard of living, as measured by median household income, has actually suffered.

Given the clear evidence that trade deals have not improved our standard of living, why do we continue to pursue them? One of the standard arguments in support of trade deals is based on the economist David Ricardo's theory of competitive advantage. In a nutshell, it says that if you produce X efficiently and I produce Y efficiently, then I shouldn't waste my labor producing X, and you shouldn't waste your labor producing Y. If each of us does what we do most efficiently, then we can trade X for Y (and vice versa), and we'll both be better off in the long run.

It's a tidy theory, but when Ricardo developed it, he presupposed perfect competition and undistorted markets—neither of which exists when it comes to our trading relationship with China, the country from which we import most of our finished goods. When China lets its currency reach market value, protects intellectual property, invests in the manufacturing costs required to make goods that comply with CPSIA and FDA guidelines, and adequately protects the health and safety of workers, then we will be nearing the state of undistorted markets under which the comparative advantage argument might be considered. There is nothing wrong with a trade agreement between two parties that play by the same—or even similar—rules. But that's not the case with China, and it's not the case with other low-cost manufacturing countries.

The latest trade deal that should have all small to midsize US manufacturers on edge is the Trans-Pacific Partnership (TPP). This is an agreement currently being negotiated among the United States, Australia, Brunei, Canada, Chile, Japan, Malaysia, Mexico, New Zealand, Peru, Singapore, and Vietnam. Note that China is not on the list. It's ironic that one of the main arguments in support of TPP is that it will help counterbalance the influence of China in the Pacific Rim. Of course, China's influence in that area of the world is to a great degree due to our support of their entry into the WTO, our massive imports of China-made goods, and their buying of our debt. In other words, TPP is a trade deal that attempts to solve a problem created by a bad trade deal.

One of the greatest dangers of TPP is its potential effect on the nascent apparel manufacturing renaissance in the United States In his presentation at the spring 2014 meeting of the Americas Apparel Producers Network, Roger Gilmartin, Managing Director of O'Rourke Group Partners, an international management consulting firm, estimated that if TPP passes, US job losses in the apparel industry alone would number 150,000 if the yarn-forward rule is eliminated. The yarn-forward rule requires that everything from the yarn to the fabric to the cut and sew operations be sourced from signatory countries. If the yarn-forward rule is negotiated away by the United States, Vietnam, which is becoming a major exporter of apparel to the United States, would be allowed to source its fabric from China. This would, in effect, give China a duty-free backdoor into the US apparel market. And let's keep in mind that even without TPP, our trade deficit with Vietnam is already surging, from $16 billion in 2012, to $20 billion in 2013, to $25 billion in 2014.

TPP could also lead to a loosening of our safety standards on imported meat and other foods. According to a June 2014 report from Public Citizen, if the TPP-member exporting country claims that their safety processes and standards are "equivalent" to those in the United States and the United States refuses entry of their goods, the exporter could bring a challenge to an international tribunal that would rule on whether the United States violated the treaty's protocol.[111] In essence, we could be dangerously dumbing down our food safety standards. Further cause for concern is that the FDA has continuously cited seafood exporters in both Vietnam and Malaysia for selling products that contain contaminants. During the five-year period from 2007 to 2012, the FDA rejected 1,380 shipments of Vietnamese seafood.[112] According to Public Citizen, the FDA has placed 192 Vietnamese fisheries on a "red list" due to risk of salmonella contamination.[113]

And finally, one of the gravest downsides to TPP is that it was negotiated totally behind closed doors. There were, of course, lobbyists that were acting as advisors to the negotiating team, but I guarantee there was no one on that list representing small to midsize manufacturers. When it comes down to the final hours of negotiations and some constituency has to be thrown under the bus, my guess was that it would once again be US manufacturers. And, according to at least one analysis of the final draft, that's exactly what happened.

Shortly after the text of the TPP deal was released, an article in the Wall Street Journal cited an analysis from the Peterson Institute for International Economics projecting that the agreement will lead to an additional $10 billion *deficit* in US heavy manufacturing, and an additional $22.8 billion *deficit* in light manufacturing.[114]

So, how are skewed trade deals passed by Congress? In the past, trade promotion authority (TPA) has been used to grease the skids. Congress periodically grants the president this authority—sometimes called "fast track"—when negotiating trade deals. In June 2015, after two weeks of intense lobbying on both sides of the aisle, Congress granted Obama trade promotion authority, which will impact both TPP and TTIP, a pending trade agreement with several European countries. Fast track is helpful to expeditious passing of trade deals because it prevents Congress from picking the deal apart. After the negotiated deal is presented, they have a simple "yes" or "no" vote. Trade negotiators claim that without TPA, negotiators from other countries won't make final concessions because the deal hammered out by the US negotiators may be amended by Congress. The clear downside to TPA, particularly in regards to the Trans-Pacific Partnership, is that the trade negotiations were held behind closed doors, which means Congress may not have adequate time for due diligence on the treaty's details before casting a vote.

I'm not necessarily against fast track, but it seems to me that the administration cannot have it both ways. If it wants fast track authority, then Congress should be kept apprised of the details of trade negotiations as they progress. If an administration negotiating a trade deal wants to keep the negotiations secret, then no TPA. Proponents of TPP and fast track authority will claim that it's not that simple. Again, this is not complicated; it's common sense. Unfortunately that ship has already sailed on TPP and TTIP

In his January 2015 State of the Union address, Obama admitted that past trade deals didn't work out well, but then asked for fast track authority while assuring that his trade deals (TPP, TTIP) would produce better results. So, we were being asked to take the administration at their word that this is a fair agreement without knowing its details, and Congress had already granted fast track authority before anyone had seen the final text of the deal. Seems to me Obama should have listened to his own advice concerning Cuba that he gave in the same speech: "When what you're doing doesn't work for 50 years, it's time to do something else." Amen, Mr. President. Since fast tracked trade deals didn't work out well for US families for the last fifty years, let's try something else.

Speaking of Cuba, it is an excellent example of our contorted and often contradictory trade policies. We are being told that it will take a few years to normalize trade relations with Cuba—a tiny island country that is, on its own, absolutely no strategic threat to the United States—because they are a Communist country that abuses human rights. Fair enough. Yet we import billions of dollars of goods from China, a Communist country that abuses human rights *and* is a serious strategic threat to US interests across the globe. Why the double standard? Incredibly, C. Fred Bergsten, a former assistant secretary of the Treasury, cowrote an op-ed piece in the *Wall Street Journal* in December 2014 actually encouraging a free-trade deal with China.[115] Am I missing something? Perhaps some politician in Washington, DC, can explain this double standard to me—or maybe not.

2. Drop the Illusion that Trade Will Weaken China as a Strategic Threat.

The China/Cuba double standard illustrates that in the quest to trade with China, some are losing sight of the fact that China remains a serious strategic threat to US interests. That threat is most clearly spelled out in a November 2014 Report to Congress prepared by the US-China Economic and Security Review Commission. The commission's mandate, by law, is to monitor, investigate, and report to Congress on the national security implications of the economic relationship between the United States and China. The exhaustive report covers the current state of China's trade, security, technology, and proliferation practices. Some of the report's conclusions are:

- Since China joined the WTO, the United States has lost 29 percent of its manufacturing jobs, and economists are beginning to establish correlations between the job loss and our trade relationship with China.
- Through subsidization, favoritism, and the practice of limiting US direct foreign investment in certain types of manufacturing, China has indirectly contributed to manufacturing job loss in the United States. Although China pledged market reforms as the price of entry into WTO, those reforms have slowed or stalled, and some government practices violate the spirit and the letter of China WTO commitments.
- China is neither a market economy, nor is it on the path of becoming one.
- Adequate trade remedies are not available for smaller US companies adversely affected by China's trade policies.
- China's manipulation of its currency serves as a subsidy for its manufacturing exporters, and US law does not provide a "sufficient remedy" for private US companies.[116]

The report goes on to detail the military threat that China poses for the United States, noting that the regional balance of power is shifting in China's direction. Further, their rapid militarization is being facilitated by the acquisition of foreign technology "through both purchase and theft."[117]

According to the same commission, not much has improved since November 2014. In their 2015 report, the commission notes that President Xi Jinping is resorting to the same old tricks – currency manipulation, government subsidies for favored industries, and excessive intervention in the financial system - as the Chinese economy sputters.[118] Two new warning bells of note in this latest report are China's bellicose actions in the South China Sea[119] and its state-sponsored cyberespionage against private U.S. companies and individuals.[120]

In his fine book *Strategic Capitalism*, Richard D'Aveni details how China has created a form of managed capitalism that provides them greater strategic flexibility to exploit what he calls the "muddle" of America's "generic capitalism."[121] He writes that the Chinese state's coordination of this brand of capitalism, including the direction of state-owned enterprises (SOEs), which make up 40 percent of China's GDP, provides them the wherewithal to pursue what is in the best interests of China as a nation as opposed to what is in the best interests of its citizens.

Consider the rampant pollution caused by China's rapid industrialization. The government simply determined that the need for industrialization was more important than the quality of the air its citizens breathe either in or outside the workplace. So pollution regulations were lax and their enforcement virtually ignored for over twenty years.

Another example of China's managed capitalism is the recently introduced rules on foreign technology companies in China. Their government is concerned that US technology companies have too much information on Chinese companies, so they simply create new rules that would force US technology companies doing business in China to "turn over secret code, submit to invasive audits and build so-called back doors into hardware and software."[122] Clearly the new rules are designed to strengthen the hand of domestic Chinese technology companies at the expense of overseas vendors. How has the US government responded to the flood of imports from China that has cost us millions of jobs? Apparently Beltway politicians simply consider it a fait accompli, and we look to do more trade deals with other countries instead of responding to China in kind.

Current and future administrations must stop operating under the illusion that if we continue to trade more with a country like China, we will all eventually sit around a campfire singing "Kumbaya." Because they play the game by different rules, more trade with China does not make them less of a strategic threat.

3. Brand China a Currency Manipulator.

As recently as the spring of 2014, in a bid to boost exports during an economic slowdown and to rein in currency speculators, China pushed the yuan sharply lower against the dollar. *Sourcing Journal Online* noted "what is now a matter of established fact is that the currency slide is not the result of unmanaged market forces but was rather intentionally engineered by China's central bank."[123] In response, the then-newly named chairman of the Senate Finance Committee, Ron Wyden (D-OR), remarked in a speech that trade agreements "must combat the new breed of predatory practices that distort trade and investment and cost American jobs." Among the practices he cited was currency manipulation. No action was taken.[124]

It's an accepted fact that China keeps its currency artificially weak against the dollar in order to keep the prices of China manufactured goods artificially low in the United States This places US manufacturers at a serious competitive disadvantage, as some economists have estimated that the yuan is as much as 40 percent undervalued against the US dollar. Thus, China manufacturers begin with a 40 percent pricing advantage over our domestic manufacturers. Add in the discount of not needing to adhere to strict environmental or safety regulations, and clearly the playing field is wildly tilted in favor of China. And China continues to manipulate their currency when it looks as though the gradually strengthening yuan will cost it US market share.

For example, after 2005, when China dropped its peg to the dollar, the yuan was gradually strengthening. Then came the Great Recession. From July 2008 through May 2010, the Chinese government prevented further appreciation of the yuan by pegging it against the dollar so that the price of Chinese goods in the United States would not increase during the downturn. On July 28, 2008, the yuan closed at 6.82 yuan per dollar. On May 24, 2010, it closed at 6.83. In the nearly two-year interim, its value barely fluctuated. Basically, China didn't want its manufacturers to lose US market share. It's no coincidence that the slow upward march of China's currency flat-lined during that period; it was manipulated to do so.

Fast-forward to August 2015. Amid a sharp factory slowdown and a free-falling domestic stock market, China suddenly devalued the yuan over a three-day period by almost 5 percent. The 1.9 percent drop on the first day constituted the largest one-day drop in the currency's value since China ended its dual currency system in 1994. Virtually overnight, China manufacturers gained a 5 percent pricing advantage over US manufacturers. The US response? Muted at best.

In spite of jawboning from presidents, Treasury secretaries, and members of Congress, at the end of the day, we take no action. As noted in an earlier chapter, the Beltway strategy seems to be for Congress to play the bad cop and the administration the good cop. This does have the effect of keeping upward pressure on the yuan, but it still remains significantly undervalued, giving China manufacturers an unfair advantage.

The big stick held by Washington is the possibility of branding China a currency manipulator. Naming China a currency manipulator would open the door to higher tariffs and other penalties on goods imported from China. There are several arguments against this course of action. One is that China is not the only country that is manipulating its currency. That may be true, but China is the only one of those countries that has a massive trade deficit with the United States.

Another argument against applying the currency manipulator tag is that the existing game of good cop/bad cop is working. Since dropping its peg to the dollar in 2005, the yuan has strengthened from 8.27 to 6.39 after China's August 2015 devaluation. Some question why we should rock the boat if the current degree of pressure is having the desired effect. However, keep in mind that the yuan has strengthened a total of only 20 percent over the course of ten years. That's progress, but it still leaves the yuan significantly undervalued. The longer we wait to force China's hand, the more our domestic supply chains, many already on life support, wither and die.

Others have said that instead of branding China a currency manipulator, we should simply weaken the dollar. But why weaken the dollar artificially in relation to all currencies when our issue is with China specifically? For the most part, the dollar is at market value against other foreign currencies. China should allow its currency to reach market value instead of the United States manipulating the value of the dollar against all currencies.

During the 2012 presidential campaign, Mitt Romney asserted that China should be branded a currency manipulator. If he had been elected and did not follow through on the threat, he would not have been the first president to espouse that line during the campaign and then backtrack after elected. It's a popular campaign position that is conveniently forgotten after the inauguration. Will the 2016 candidates do the same? Probably. But one thing is certain—the People's Bank of China will continue to walk a fine line, trying to keep the appreciation of the yuan as slow as possible when their economy is humming and flat or down when their economy sputters, maintaining the advantage for their manufacturers. It's time for a US administration to move beyond the rhetoric and the good cop/bad cop game and do something palpable to help our manufacturers by branding China a currency manipulator.

4. Don't Weaken Buy American Laws—Strengthen Them.

For the tenth anniversary of the September 11 terrorist attack, the U.S. Transportation and Security Administration purchased seventy thousand commemorative bracelets to give to their employees as a tribute to those who died in the tragedy. The bracelets were made in China and purchased under an exemption from legislation that was passed to ensure the government buys from US manufacturers.[125]

Most people don't know that the federal government has signed trade agreements—including the Government Procurement Agreement of the WTO—that supersede state-level Buy American legislation. What is Buy American legislation? It is legislation passed by state governments which requires state agencies to grant a preference to US products or services when putting a project out for bid. A number of states already have such laws, and the concept is a reasonable one. Does it mean that all state purchases will be US-made goods or services? No, but it helps.

In return for allowing US companies access to government contracts in other countries, past trade agreements have granted overseas companies access to US federal and state government contracts. This federal trade policy trumps state laws. In fact, some state-level Buy American legislation carries wording that the state preference for US-made cannot supersede federal law. Fortunately, foreign companies purposely blocked from state bids by Buy American laws have no direct recourse in US courts. Only the federal government can take such action, and it is highly unlikely that it would.[126]

At a federal level, there are three laws that require US government purchasing agents to give a preference to US manufacturers—the Buy American Act, the Berry Amendment, and the Buy America Act. The Buy American Act, passed in 1933, is the most wide-ranging domestic preference statute of the three. The Berry Amendment is related exclusively to purchases by the Department of Defense. The Buy America Act (not to be confused with the Buy American Act) applies only to mass transit projects funded at least partly by federal grants with a value of over $100,000. All three require that a preference be given to domestic manufacturers, but all have provisions that allow for foreign sourcing when a US alternative is either unavailable or too expensive.

Given these provisions, one wonders why the power of federal, state, and local governments to establish a preference for US-made products and services in government bids would be traded away as a concession in international trade deals. I realize the horse may have already left the barn on this one, but government should be *extending* these types of preferences, not trimming them. Not only does Buy American legislation create or maintain US jobs; it also sends the message that our federal, state, and local governments value US manufacturing. And even if only a limited percentage of state government purchases stay in the United States because of these laws, then it is business worth having for US manufacturers.

In spite of the obvious benefits, constituencies opposed to Buy American laws make strikingly similar arguments against them. Here is a recap of the arguments typically made—and why those arguments are wrong.

Argument #1: Buying American would raise the costs of the project.

Perhaps, but we must also consider the *total* cost to the city, state, or federal government. If the price to the government entity for the Buy American project is X percent higher, is that X percent premium covered by the taxes paid by the US workers employed because of the Buy American provision? Conversely, if those jobs are lost due to the lack of the Buy American provision, what is the cost to the government entity of unemployment and other benefits?

Thus, although the *price* of the project may be higher, the difference between the higher price and the *actual cost* to government may be ameliorated, or eliminated, by these other factors.

Argument #2: It's impractical—some intermediate parts may not be available here in the United States.

Yes, that's possible in some cases. However, both the Berry Amendment and Buy American Act have loopholes that allow federal government agencies to buy overseas if the price from US vendors is too high or the product is not available domestically. And these waivers are used often. In a report released by Senator Chris Murphy (D-CT) in May 2015, it was reported that the Department of Defense alone had granted over 307,000 waivers to the Buy American Act between 2007 and 2015, amounting to over $176 billion in purchases. Most of the waivers were granted because the products purchased were to be used overseas.[127]

As for the Berry Amendment, a loophole already exists that allows the Department of Defense to buy outside the United States if the value of the contract is below $150,000. One of the dirty little secrets of government procurement is that purchasing agents will sometimes split one large contract into several smaller contracts—each below the $150,000 threshold—to avoid the need to source from a US manufacturer. Given wriggle room like this, can one really believe that it's impractical to buy American?

Argument #3: Since working conditions are deplorable in most low-cost manufacturing countries, by buying there we help create better living conditions for the jobless in those countries.

This is a public relations argument often used by multinational manufacturers, brands, and big-box retailers to justify offshoring. It's ironic when large corporations characterize their sourcing model as a form of philanthropy for developing nations, when what the sourcing model truly reflects is the slogan "always the low price." For example, it's apparent that apparel importers started sourcing in Bangladesh not to help the Bangladeshi people, but to buy at the lowest possible price. It is only since the tragedies of the Tazreen factory fire and Rana Plaza building collapse that those same companies are now touting their sense of "social responsibility" for the people of Bangladesh as the reason for not moving their apparel purchases to another country (or back to the United States).

Of course, anyone with a shred of empathy is concerned about the poor in developing countries. But should that concern drive government purchasing policies? Should US government procurement be a form of social welfare for other countries? Is that not the role of foreign aid?

Argument #4: We should let the free market rule and buy where the goods are cheapest. In the long run, it's better for all.

See my previous comments concerning Ricardo's theory of competitive advantage. It's a great theory—in a perfect world. Let us also remember that China is a strategic threat to the United States, so the trade policy tail should not be wagging the foreign policy dog.

Argument #5: Government preference for "Made in the USA" is protectionist trade policy; China cites Buy American rules as justification for their own discriminatory policies.

This is a spin-off from the "comparative advantage" argument, often used by multinationals more interested in selling into China than rocking the boat with China. If China didn't have Buy American laws as an excuse for their own trade barriers, they would find another whipping boy.

Argument #6: If it's good to buy U.S.A.-made, isn't it even better to buy Texas-made? And if it's good to buy Texas-made, isn't it better still to be Dallas-made, and so on?

Hoover Institution economist David Henderson actually made this weak reductio ad absurdum argument for a John Stossel column written in November 2011.[128] Why is it weak? Because the debatable proposition is not whether it is good to buy "Made in the U.S.A."; rather, it's whether it is in the best interest of the United States and its citizens for US government purchasing policy to establish a preference for products made in the United States of America under reasonable circumstances. This is a more nuanced proposition than the one set up by Henderson.

There is no downside to government-mandated Buy American laws as long as that mandate ensures flexibility if the comparable US product is much more expensive or simply not available here in the United States. Sadly, the point may soon be moot. The Trans-Pacific Partnership trade agreement currently being negotiated may add a number of low-cost manufacturing countries in the Pacific Rim to the list of nations that are not subject to Buy American laws.

To add insult to injury, when the fiscal year 2016 National Defense Authorization Act was unveiled in the House in spring 2015, the proposed bill that came out of committee raised the simplified acquisition threshold for Berry Amendment purchases from $150,000 to $500,000. Instead of all Department of Defense purchases over $150,000 being subject to the Berry Amendment, the new threshold would allow any purchase below $500,000 to be open to imports, creating potentially serious consequences for many smaller US manufacturers who rely on defense contracts. I was personally involved, along with other members of the Narrow Fabrics Institute[129], in the lobbying effort in the House that reversed this decision and remain involved in attempting to change the Senate version of the bill that also contains the increased threshold. Only time will tell if our efforts are successful. Remarkably, I have seen no metrics during this process that show how raising the threshold would provide any savings for the Department of Defense.

5. Ramp Up Port Inspections.

Lumber Liquidators is one of the largest providers of flooring for homes and businesses in the United States. On March 1, 2015, a segment on the CBS News program *60 Minutes* reported that laminated flooring purchased from Lumber Liquidators and installed in possibly as many as hundreds of thousands of homes contained formaldehyde levels twenty times over the legal limit. Children are the most likely to be affected by these high levels of formaldehyde. The laminated flooring was made in China.

Chapter 6 dealt with the importance of making *finer* product to more effectively compete with overseas competitors. However, government also has a role to play on this issue. US manufacturers jump through a number of regulatory hoops to ensure that their products meet government-mandated guidelines for product safety. Yet the government agencies that are tasked with ensuring that unsafe imports do not reach the consumer are able to test only a small percentage of the food and products that arrive at our ports from overseas.

According to the Consumer Products Safety Commission (CPSC) budget request for fiscal year 2016, more than 80 percent of consumer product recalls in 2013 involved imported product. A total of $723 billion in products under CPSC's jurisdiction—nearly $2 billion per day—were imported into the United States during that same year. Yet the CPSC staffs fewer than 5 percent of US ports. The CPSC admits that they have neither an adequate number of product inspectors at ports nor the computer targeting systems that would allow them to better identify noncompliant products.

In their fiscal year 2016 budget request, the CPSC asked for fifty additional inspectors and an improved technology targeting system that would allow them to "analyze 100 percent of incoming import product lines under the CPSC's jurisdiction and designate high-risk entries before those imports reach U.S. ports ..." Total estimated cost for the program was $36 million. Seems like a bargain to me. These requests should be granted not only to ensure that unsafe imported products don't make it to our store shelves, but also to help level the playing field for US manufacturers. Overseas companies know they have a good chance of beating the odds when they ship unsafe products into our country. Let's change the odds in our favor by adequately funding CPSC port inspections.

Inspection of imported food is perhaps an even bigger problem. In October 2012, Bloomberg News reported on shrimp from Vietnam, headed eventually to the United States, being stored in dirty plastic vats filled with ice made from tap water that even the Vietnamese Health Ministry states should be boiled before drinking. The same story described tilapia from China that had been partly fed with feces from pigs and geese.[130] Yet less than 2 percent of all food brought into the country is physically inspected.

In its budget request for fiscal year 2016, the FDA asked for a $109.5 million increase in its budget to enhance oversight of both domestic and overseas companies. Clearly Congress will go over that request with a fine-tooth comb. When it comes time to make the inevitable cuts in the budget request, funding for the inspection of imported food should be maintained or increased.

6. Stop Trying to Pick "Winning" Industries.

In the fall of 2010, former Red Sox pitcher Curt Schilling and his start-up video company, 38 Studios, were lured from Massachusetts to Rhode Island with a $75 million loan from the state's Economic Development Corporation. A press release from the governor's office read: "38 Studios presents Rhode Island with a tremendous economic development opportunity. This investment creates 450 high-paying jobs, provides job opportunities for our college graduates in a fast growing industry, and will attract other interactive and entertainment companies to Rhode Island." By May 2012 the company had collapsed, and the state of Rhode Island was on the hook for as much as $112 million.[131]

The 38 Studios deal is a near-perfect example of why government economic development efforts should not be focused on selecting companies in particular industries that are considered "advanced" or high tech. There were, no doubt, a number of small to midsize manufacturing companies in Rhode Island that could have used a small piece of that $75 million to expand their facilities and hire more employees. But economic development efforts always seem to focus on the brass ring of "advanced" industries. During the time that the 38 Studios deal was imploding, I was aware of a Rhode Island manufacturer—with a multimillion-dollar order in hand from a big-box retailer—who could not get a loan to expand his factory. Clearly, a better bet for the Rhode Island EDC would have been to make a loan one-tenth the size of the 38 Studios loan to this company. I suspect they didn't think their product was glamorous enough.

And if you think the federal government can do a better job at picking winners, the Solyndra debacle proves otherwise. In 2009 the US Energy Department provided the California-based manufacturer of solar panels with a $536 million loan guarantee to build a new fabrication plant that would employ hundreds. By August 2011 the company had filed for chapter 11 bankruptcy protection. The government recouped some of the investment, but $385 million was lost. Records showed that as the company was spiraling downward, politicians in DC were more concerned with the political fallout than with the massive loss of jobs.[132]

It is apparent that government typically does a poor job of picking winners when it comes to loaning money to companies in "advanced" industries. Yet in the triumph of hope over experience, they continue to try. Meanwhile smaller companies in basic manufacturing industries have trouble getting modest loans. This isn't to say that companies in high-tech industries should not be supported; only that economic development efforts should not slight basic manufacturing in favor of high-tech industries. In fact, they shouldn't look at industry at all.

Government-sponsored economic development efforts should focus less on industry and more on business model. For example, it's safer to place a small bet on a basic manufacturer that understands the principles of *fewer, faster,* and *finer* than to place a large bet on a company in an advanced industry. Every city and town in every state in this country is looking to corral that glamorous high-tech company, and it's tempting to swing for the fences. But if state and local governments really want to help manufacturers, they should look for solid singles and doubles hitters, regardless of the industry—especially if that midsize manufacturer has implemented *fewer, faster,* and *finer*.

7. Invest in Education and Infrastructure.

Winter 2015 was particularly tough in Rhode Island, and one of its main side effects—potholes—shines a light on the dismal state of our country's infrastructure. A 2013 report card on America's infrastructure, prepared by the American Society of Civil Engineers, graded our bridges at C+, noting that one in nine of our roadway bridges is structurally deficient and that the average age of the over six hundred thousand bridges in this country is forty-two years. Inland waterways, which carry the equivalent of fifty-one million truck trips each year, received a D- grade due to the generally poor condition of locks and channels that need dredging. The condition of our roads was graded D, transit systems D, energy grid D+, and aviation D. Because the state of our infrastructure has a direct relationship with our ability to compete globally, it must be addressed. Aging infrastructure is a sure sign that we have lost our edge as a world leader.[133]

In a document prepared for the American Road and Transportation Builders Association, James Pinkerton and Bob Patterson make a compelling case for the past and future importance of government-funded infrastructure. They take the reader through the historical and political figures, from George Washington to Dwight D. Eisenhower, who had the vision and tenacity to ensure that the United States had the world's best waterways, railroads, and highways. And they take us through the slow steady decline since the 1970s, linking our deteriorating infrastructure with the loss of manufacturing jobs.

Pinkerton and Patterson note that "perhaps the most far-reaching consequence of the collapse of U.S infrastructure has been the corresponding loss of manufacturing jobs and the waning of America's middle class. When a country scrimps on infrastructure, or kills big public projects, it also sidelines its manufacturing sector. That overlooked side effect has weakened America by marginalizing the 65 percent of the U.S. workforce without college degrees, whose livelihoods, since the days of Henry Ford, have largely depended on making material things."[134]

Meanwhile, in the American Society of Civil Engineers report, the conditions of our public schools facilities received a D grade. Much has been written about the "knowledge gap" between available jobs and the unemployed, and that gap must be bridged. Bridging it begins with a better school environment. As a nation, we will never produce better students until we provide better school buildings, better equipment, and a clean, safe environment in which to learn.

In many respects, developments in the high-technology sector of our economy have blinded us to the dangers of our crumbling infrastructure. Garry Kasparov and Silicon Valley investor Peter Thiel, in a 2012 *Financial Times* op-ed, wrote that "we can now use our phones to send cute kitten photos around the world or watch episodes of The Jetsons while riding a century-old subway; we can programme software to simulate futuristic landscapes. But the actual landscape around us is almost identical to the 1960s."[135]

8. Encourage Corporate Patriotism.

In August 2014 the Walgreens store chain announced that they were going to complete their purchase of a smaller European rival and move their corporate headquarters to Switzerland in order to take advantage of the European country's lower tax rate. Public reaction, largely fueled by social media, was swift and vehemently opposed to the strategy. Days after the announcement, Walgreens reversed course and decided against the maneuver, known as a tax inversion.

In a tax inversion deal, a US company acquires a (usually) smaller company in another country with lower tax rates, "merges" with that company, and moves its nominal headquarters to the lower tax country. It's not illegal. However, if a US-based company does a tax inversion deal—which helps them avoid US taxes—should they still be considered a US company? Not in my book. They may still market themselves as though they are a US company, but if your headquarters isn't in the United States, you're no longer a US company. What spiked the social media uproar was that Walgreens had traditionally positioned itself as a "Main Street U.S.A." company and would have certainly continued to do so after the financial maneuver.

Walgreens's decision to forgo its tax inversion was, in many ways, a big win for the Made in the U.S.A. movement. I'm guessing that Walgreens's board and management were spooked by the social media backlash that ensued from their announcement. That backlash was enabled (and ennobled) by the entire Made in the U.S.A. movement, which rallied a critical mass of Main Street Americans who resent it when multinational companies drape the American flag over their shoulders while offshoring jobs and seeking overseas tax havens. Of course, there is nothing illegal about tax inversions or offshoring; just don't take those actions while marketing your company as a Main Street American brand and expect folks in the Made in the U.S.A. movement to swallow it. We aren't that naive—and we're clearly not shy about whipping up a storm.

Shortly after the adverse publicity of the Walgreens saga, the Obama administration tightened tax rules to make tax inversions less lucrative and more difficult to execute. He or the next president might also consider taking a tip from *Strategic Capitalism* and champion what Richard D'Aveni calls "corporate patriotism."[136] D'Aveni notes that in the push toward globalization, we have lost sight of placing national needs over corporate needs. Present and future administrations should consider using their bully pulpit to help reverse that trend.

Government will never be *the* answer to regaining our edge as manufacturers. Policies and programs change with each administration, and there is no consistent overarching plan. But government can take the above eight steps to provide small to midsize manufacturers a business environment less skewed in favor of overseas competitors. Just give us something approaching a level playing field, Washington, DC, and we'll take care of the rest.

CONCLUSION

The Recession-Proof Business

Trans-Tex had two major domestic competitors. Within the span of eight months straddling the fall of 2014 and the summer of 2015, one filed for chapter 7 bankruptcy, and we acquired the other. The first never really grasped how the world had changed and, thus, never understood how the concepts of *fewer, faster,* and *finer* could help them to respond. The second understood the importance of the principles but did not have people with the skills to implement them. The success of Trans-Tex—double-digit growth throughout the depths of the Great Recession and quadrupling in volume during the worst economic environment since the 1930s—was driven by the ascendant business model of *fewer, faster,* and *finer*. While our competitors were struggling in an old-school industry that was itself struggling, we were thriving.

If you are a manufacturer and you want to be prepared for the inevitable next recession, start implementing the principles of *fewer, faster,* and *finer* in your manufacturing operation today. History shows that we average an economic downturn or a recession about once every eight to ten years—early 80s, early 90s, early 00s. The Great Recession arrived a little early, which means that we are highly likely to see another downturn before the end of this decade. As the economy turns downward, B2B buyers will be even more pressured than they are today to keep inventories low, and their response will be to demand lower order quantities delivered more quickly. And if retail consumers have less money to spend, they'll spend it on the exact product they want that can be delivered exactly when they want it—and the quality had better be exactly what they expect, or your brand will face an immediate social media backlash.

After you have implemented the principles of *fewer*, *faster*, and *finer* in your manufacturing operation, it's time to market those capabilities to take US customers back from overseas competitors. The following is the profile of a US customer/prospect that would be highly receptive to the *fewer*, *faster*, and *finer* business model:

- US-based, currently buying imported product
- Prefers to maintain low inventory levels
- Needs small average order size and/or product customization
- Needs expedited production lead times
- Quality and safety are an issue
- Their current overseas source could/did sell around them

To sell the *fewer*, *faster*, and *finer* model, show how your overseas competitors compare with your company for minimum order size, production lead times (including the shipping time), and product quality and safety. These comparisons should be based on clearly measurable criteria.

Do not hesitate to sell fear. It's likely that your US prospect is concerned about the safety record of imported products and the propensity of overseas sources—whether inadvertently or purposely—to sell around them to their customers. Use this concern to highlight your company's loyalty to the distribution channel. Make certain your US prospect knows that you will never bypass them and sell around them, and be willing to prove it even at your own short-term expense.

If you have test results on product safety from certified labs, use them in your presentation. Make sure your customer knows that if a China source will ship lead-tainted children's toys to Mattel, they will not hesitate to send poor quality or unsafe product to them if it is to the China manufacturer's advantage.

If you are the CEO, president, or owner of the company, jump on a plane—*often*—to visit US customers and prospects currently buying imports. You will likely find that they do not relish buying overseas; they simply feel they have no other choice. Give them clear, measurable reasons to give that business to you instead.

We must keep in mind that the second American industrial revolution will not be driven by the practices that made our nation a manufacturing juggernaut sixty-five years ago. Those conditions cannot be recreated. Back then, our potential overseas manufacturing competitors were located in countries devastated by World War II. Other less developed countries had not yet created manufacturing capacity, much less the infrastructure to support it. We were the king of the hill because we were the only country that could service demand in a recovering global economy. To service that demand we perfected the concept of long production runs of commodity-type products.

But the days of being successful in this country by manufacturing long runs of commodity products at the lowest possible price are over. That skill is now transportable, so as costs rise in China, that type of business will migrate to Bangladesh, India, Vietnam, or Africa. Other countries are building the infrastructure, creating the capacity, and mastering the science. Perhaps long production runs of cheap products can be one leg of a domestic manufacturer's business model, but it cannot be—and should not be—the only one. The world has changed; the customer has changed. Acknowledge that change, embrace it, and prepare your business to adapt.

The demand for mass customization, speed to market, and better quality are here to stay. In fact, one could argue that they are a natural by-product of a mature industrial economy and that they will inevitably lead to more localized manufacturing across the globe. Which means that European or Australian manufacturers battling with low-cost imports could learn from the principles of *fewer*, *faster*, and *finer*. And those protectionist barriers that China constructs to keep US firms out? If they simply shifted their manufacturing business model to incorporate these principles, they would be better able to service their domestic customers with products and service that delight.

I have been accused in some circles of bashing China. In fact, there were some US manufacturing executives who wholeheartedly agree with my message but did not want their story to appear here or asked that their company name be changed, because they hope to sell into China and are concerned they might be blackballed. I even had a phone meeting with an editor at one publishing company who asked me if I could dial down the China rhetoric because they sell so many books in China. But this book is not about bashing China, nor is it about denigrating foreign companies or foreign workers. If today's competition comes from China, tomorrow's will come from the latest in what will be a long line of low-cost manufacturing countries. This book is about my experience with the US manufacturing worker, those people cheering on the factory floor of that small company in Cranston, Rhode Island, and the millions of others across the United States. They are my team. I wrote this book in hopes of coaching them and their companies about how to take down a tough low-cost overseas competitor without depending solely on government protection.

If US manufacturing is to continue its renaissance, we cannot wait for government to act. We cannot depend on government set-aside programs, defense contracts, or the imposition of highly regulated markets. Local, state, and national policies can provide a limited degree of assistance, but they will never be sufficient to ensure long-term success. Government policies cannot change the tides of globalization; they can only help us cope in relatively small ways for a limited period of time. Those policies can (and have) actually hurt us a lot, and they can only help us a little. It is up to us as business leaders to reinvent our older companies, creating new companies to better respond to market conditions in a global economy with a changing customer.

Our success, even during the deepest economic recession, will be ensured by creating products that are safe to use and delight the customer, by focusing on smaller, more customized production runs, and by delivering those products exactly when and where the customer wants them. No matter what type of manufacturing business you run, where it's located, or from what countries your low-cost competition originates, integrating the concepts of *fewer, faster,* and *finer* into your operation will raise the bar for your competition, particularly overseas competition, ensure your success, and make your employees and your customers cheer.

AMERICAN DRAGON

Follow *American Dragon* on Facebook and Twitter

Visit the *American Dragon* Website:
www.americandragon.us

Visit the *American Dragon* Blog:
https://americandragonblogs.wordpress.com/

INDEX

38 Studios
   demise of 152

A

Adidas 5
Amaras Law
   3-D printing, proliferation of 61
Amazon
   drones, use of for delivery 73
American Airlines 24
American Locomotive Works (ALCO) 48
American Society of Civil Engineers
   US infrastructure, 2013 report on 153
Anderson, Fran 113
Apple 47
Asian Development Bank 4
Atchison Products
   offshoring of manufacturing 93
A. T. Cross 24, 30
AT&T 24

B

Bangladesh xiv, 45, 74
   forced labor in 132
   supply chain disruption in 76
Barr, Phil 49, 68, 81, 121
Barton Company 12
Bassett Furniture
   strategy to combat China imports 59
Beltre, Matilde 116
Benoit, Isabelle xvii, xviii, 41
Bergsten, C. Fred 141

Betaspring 70
Boston Consulting Group
   shrinking pricing advantage of China manufacturers 3
   wage increases in China 4
Bouchard, Herb 111
Brenner, Rick 100
Bullet Blues xvii, 41
Burma
   forced labor in 132
Burnett, Matthew
   Makers Row, founding of 130

C

California Proposition 65
   effect on manufacturers 94
Canada Federal Trade Commission
   intellectual property protection in China 16
Capitol Cups 99
Cary, Paul 111
Chafee, Lincoln 26
China
   as strategic threat to the U.S. 141
   currency manipulation in 7
   demographic shifts in 4
   effect of volatile oil prices on manufacturers in 9
   pollution in 10
   real estate speculation in 11
   reduction of arable land in 10
China manufacturers
   effect of U.S. product safety

regulations on 14
vulnerabilities in business model of 2
Chung, Hannah
  Jerry the Bear, creation of 69
Clinton, President Bill 7
C. M. Offray and Son 35
Coca-Cola 24
Cochrane, Bruce 124
Committee on Foreign Relations, US Senate 26
Consumer Products Safety Commission (CPSC)
  budget request for fiscal year 2016 151
Consumer Products Safety Improvement Act 18
  effect on manufacturers of 95
Consumer Reports 26
Corrente, Jayne 110
Corrente, Paul 116
Crompton, David 1

D

Davis Industries 60
De Carvalho, Tino 117
Delta Galil 36
Disintermediation 39
Dye sublimation printing
  definition of 49

E

Edwards, Ben
  Job Shop Company, founding of 128

F

Faster principle
  definition of xv
  mind-set that necessitates implementation of 74
Federal Trade Commission
  Made in USA labeling 132
Fewer principle
  definition of xv
  mind-set that necessitates implementation of 56
Finer principle
  definition of xv
Floyd, Dana 109
Fontana, Pat 110
Food and Drug Administration (FDA)
  budget request for fiscal year 2016 151
Ford 24
Foxconn 5, 6, 47, 55, 58
Fruit of the Loom 36, 42

G

Galafassi, Antonio 16
Garland Pen Company 25
Georgia Narrow Fabrics 35
Gillette
  business model of 40
Goodwin, John 114
Greene Plastics 91, 106

H

HanesBrands
  reshoring of hosiery finishing and packaging 78
Harris, Joshua 63
Harwood Company
  effect of China price increases on 3
Hebert, Skip 49, 121
Hornbuckle, Matt 60
Horowitz, Aaron
  Jerry the Bear, creation of 69
Hughes, Raelynn
  Mommy Necklaces, founding of 90

I

India xiv, 7, 159
International Longshore and Warehouse Union (ILWU)
  West Coast port disruptions, role in 77
International Marketing Advantages 32, 51

J

Job Shop Company
  business model of 129
Jun, Lei 40
Just-A-Stretch 20, 35, 38, 40, 42, 43, 45, 108, 113, 122

K

Kegang, Liang 9

L

Laferriere, Robert, Jr. 36, 112, 116
Laferriere, Robert, Sr. 35
Lanyard
  definition of 49
Lew, Jack 8
Liberty Bottleworks
  example of fewer principle 61
Lincolnton Furniture
  demise of 124
Lipscomb, Todd
  Made in USA Forever, founding of 134
Local Motors
  3-D printed cars, production of 62
Lumber Liquidators
  formaldehyde levels in imported laminated flooring 150
Lytvinenko, Sarah and Victor
  Raleigh Denim, founding of 107

M

Made In USA Forever
  business model of 134
Makers Row
  business model of 131
Mattel
  toy recalls, 2007 95
Median household income
  stagnation of 137
MIT Taskforce on Innovation and Production 41
Mommy Necklaces
  founding of 90

Moser, Harry
  Reshoring Initiative, founding of 125

N

Narrow Fabrics Institute 150
Newell Rubbermaid 34
North American Free Trade Agreement (NAFTA) xiv, 26, 45, 133, 137, 174

O

Obama, President Barack 45

P

Pacific Maritime Association
  West Coast port disruptions, role in 77
Pinkerton, James, and Patterson, Bob
  US infrastructure, deterioration of 154
Pisano, Gary xii, xvii, 42
Promotional Products Association International (PPAI) 22
  product safety website 100
Promotional products marketplace
  hiding information in 28
  history of sourcing in 28
  production lead times in 24

Q

Quick Fitting
  reshoring, reasons for 1
quick response system
  apparel offshoring, role in 80
Quill xiv, 20, 30, 38, 40, 41, 42, 48
  history of 21
  slant-top pen design 25

R

Raleigh Denim 107
Rana Plaza 80, 149
Reebok 5
Reshoring Initiative
  role of 126

Rhode Island Economic Development
    Corporation 26
Ricardo, David
    competitive advantage theory 138

S

Sanlu Group
    tainted milk controversy, role in 97
Sareen, Raj
    offshoring, effect on apparel industry 102
Shih, Willy xii, xvii, 42
Slater, Samuel xiii, 34
Solyndra
    demise of 152
Speroni, Frank 19
Sproutel 70, 71, 72

T

TA Creations
    lunch box recall 92
Tazreen factory fire 6, 14, 80, 149
Technology/Globalization Vortex 39
Tessier, Aram 21
Textile mills
    migration of 34
Timberland 5
Total Cost of Ownership Estimator 126
Trade promotion authority (TPA)
    explanation of 140
Trans-Pacific Partnership (TPP)
    potential downsides of 138

U

Under the Dome video 10
Unilife 97
United States Boathouse Sports
   using fewer principle to compete with imports 60

United States Rubber Company 48
U.S. Block Windows
    reshoring of parts production 77
US-China Business Council 42
U.S.-China Economic and Security
    Review Commission
    report findings, November 2014 141

V

Vaughan-Bassett Company
    strategy to combat China furniture imports 59
Vibco 14, 64, 112, 114
Vietnam xiv, 7, 36, 40, 74, 76, 132, 138, 139, 151, 159

W

Wadensten, Karl
    lean principles implementation 112
Wages
    downward pressure on 120
Walgreens
    tax inversion 155
Whitt, Michael 114
World Bank
    China air pollution study, 2007 10
World Trade Organization (WTO) xiv, 43, 45, 142
Wyden, Ron 8

X

Xiaomi
    business model of 40

Y

Yount, Jacob 13

ENDNOTES

Introduction

1. Jeffrey Sparshott, "Job Gains Support Fed Plan on Rates," *Wall Street Journal*, Saturday/Sunday, August 8–9, 2015, page A1.
2. Douglas McIntyre, "China Passes the U.S. as Largest Manufacturer," *24/7 Wall Street*, March 14, 2011, http://247wallst.com/2011/03/14/china-passes-the-us-as-largest-manufacturer/.
3. Production in the Innovation Economy Commission (PIE), "A Preview of the MIT Production in the Innovation Economy Report," Massachusetts Institute of Technology, 2013, page 11.
4. Gary Pisano and Willy Shih, "Producing Prosperity," Harvard Business Review Press, Boston, MA, October 2012, page 13.

Chapter 1

5. Sun Tzu, The Art of War, translated by Thomas Cleary, Boston, MA, Shambala Publications, 1988, page 49.
6. Andy Smith, "R.I. company plans to move manufacturing to the U.S.," *Providence Journal*, March 7, 2012, page A4.
7. Penny Brooks, "Manufacturing Competitiveness: China's Exports Losing Low Cost Advantage," May 1, 2014, http://beta.tutor2u.net/business/blog/chinas-exports-losing-low-cost-advantages.
8. Tom Orlik, "Made in China Is Getting More Expensive," *Wall Street Journal*, August 11, 2012, page B16.
9. Justin Lahart and Tom Orlik, "Fade in China, Made in America," *Wall Street Journal*, March 10–11, 2012, page B16.
10. Douglas Hohner, Hal Sirkin, and Michael Zinser, "Made in America, Again—Why Manufacturing Will Return to the U.S.," Boston Consulting Group, page 3.
11. Harold Sirkin, "China vs. the U.S.: It's Just as Cheap to Make Goods in the USA," The Management Blog, Bloomberg Business, April 25, 2014.

12. Yolanda Fernandez Lommen, Asian Development Bank Briefs No. 6, October 2010, page 2.
13. Laurie Burkett, "No Baby Boom after Shift in One-Child Policy," *Wall Street Journal*, Saturday/Sunday, November 8–9, 2014, page A6.
14. Laurie Burkett, "China's Leaders Scrap One-Child Policy," *Wall Street Journal*, October 30, 2015, page A7.
15. Yolanda Fernandez Lommen, Asian Development Bank Briefs No. 6, October 2010, page 2.
16. Ross Perlin, "Chinese Workers Foxconned," Dissent, Spring 2013, https://www.dissentmagazine.org/article/chinese-workers-foxconned
17. Ibid.
18. David Barboza and Keith Bradsher, "Riot at Foxconn Factory Underscores Rift in China," New York Times, September 24, 2012, http://www.nytimes.com/2012/09/25/business/global/foxconn-riot-underscores-labor-rift-in-china.html?_r=0
19. Jonathan Kaiman, "Strike Spreads at Chinese Supplier to Adidas and Nike," The Guardian, April 22, 2014, http://www.theguardian.com/world/2014/apr/22/strike-spreads-chinese-supplier-adidas-nike-yeu-yuen-factory-jiangxi-guangdong
20. Staff, "Wage Increases in China: Should Multinationals Rethink Their Manufacturing and Sourcing Strategies," Accenture, February 2011, page 10.
21. At least 117 Bangladeshi garment workers died when a fire erupted on the ground floor of a factory in Dhaka on November 24, 2012. Many were trapped due to the lack of appropriate emergency exits from the upper floors of the building. Several jumped to their deaths from upper-story windows.
22. Jack Linshi, "Report: 168 Million Worldwide Were Laborers in 2013," October 7, 2014, http://time.com/3479472/child-labor/.
23. Doug Palmer, "U.S. says China yuan undervalued, but not manipulated," Reuters, May 27, 2011, http://www.reuters.com/article/us-usa-china-currency-idUSTRE74Q6C620110527
24. Neil Irwin, "Lew confirmation hearings for Treasury features tough questions, but few fireworks," Washington Post, February 13, 2013, https://www.washingtonpost.com/news/wonk/wp/2013/02/13/breaking-the-latest-from-jack-lews-senate-confirmation-hearing/
25. U.S. Department of Treasury, Office of Internal Affairs, "Report to Congress on International Economic and Exchange Rate Policies," April 12, 2013, page 18, www.treasury.gov/resource-center/international/exchange-rate-policies/Documents/Foreign%20Exchange%20Report%20April%202013.pdf
26. Staff, "New Senate Finance Chairman Sets Markers on Trade Policy," Sandler Travis & Rosenberg Trade Report, April 11, 2014, http://www.strtrade.com/news-publications-Wyden-trade-policy-TPA-FTA-041114.html.

27 Pedro H. Albuquerque, Joao Ricardo Faria, Miquel A. Leon-Ledisma, and Andre Varella Mollick, "China Exports and the Oil Price," http://www.kent.ac.uk/economics/documents/research/papers/2008/0812.pdf.
28 Associated Press, "Jar of French Mountain Air Sells for 512 British Pounds in Polluted Beijing," The Guardian, April 10, 2014, http://www.theguardian.com/environment/2014/apr/10/jar-french-mountain-air-polluted-beijing/print.
29 Jintai Lin, Da Pan, Steven J. Davis, Qiang Zhang, Kebin He, Can Wang, David G. Streets, Donald J. Wuebbles, and Dabo Guanc, "China's International Trade and Air Pollution in the United States," Proceedings of the National Academy of Sciences of the United States of America, January 21, 2014, http://www.ncbi.nlm.nih.gov/pmc/articles/PMC3918792/.
30 Sarah LeTrent, "Unmasking a new trend: stylish smog masks," CNN, November 2, 2014, http://www.cnn.com/2014/10/31/living/smog-mask-china-fashion-week/
31 Edward Wong, "One-Fifth of China's Farmland is Polluted, State Study Finds," New York Times, April 17, 2014, http://www.nytimes.com/2014/04/18/world/asia/one-fifth-of-chinas-farmland-is-polluted-state-report-finds.html
32 Te-Ping Chen, "Beijing Quashes Web Video on Pollution," *Wall Street Journal*, Saturday/Sunday, March 7–8, 2015, page A5.
33 Te-Ping Chen, "China Sees More Cases Against Polluters," *Wall Street Journal*, Friday, March 13, 2015, page A11.
34 17 Andrew Collier, "Failed Land Sales in China," October 9, 2014, http://www.orientcapitalresearch.com/wp-content/uploads/2014/10/Failed-Land-Sales-in-China.pdf.
35 Dye sublimation is a process whereby special inks are printed onto paper, then transferred onto fabric through a combination of heat and pressure. The dye sublimation process is often used to decorate T-shirts and other products.
36 Jacob Yount, "Chinese Factory: Like a Big Machine," www.jacobyount.com, August 14, 2012.
37 Keith Naughton, David Welch, Jeff Green, and Mina Kimes, "GM's Supplier Squeezing Days Gave Birth to Flawed Models," Bloomberg News, March 22, 2014, http://www.bloomberg.com/news/2014-03-21/gm-s-supplier-squeezing-days-gave-birth-to-flawed-models.html.
38 Staff, "The IP Commission Report – The Report of the Commission on the Theft of U.S. Intellectual Property," Published on behalf of the Commission on the Theft of American Intellectual Property by the National Bureau of Asian Research, May 2013, http://www.ipcommission.org/report/IP_Commission_Report_052213.pdf.
39 Staff, "Tramontina to Expand U.S. Manufacturing," *Gourmet Retailer*, March 13, 2013, http://www.gourmetretailer.com/top-story-housewares-_tramontina_to_expand_u.s._manufacturing-11012.html.

Chapter 2

40 Sun Tzu, The Art of War, translated by Thomas Cleary, Boston, MA, Shambala Publications, 1988, page 44.

41 The Quill Company is not to be confused with the Quill Corporation, a distributor of office supplies that was purchased by Staples in 1998.

42 Richard G. Ebel, "PPAI at 100," Promotional Products Association International, 2003, page 15.

43 Ibid., page 16.

44 Promotional Products Association International (PPAI) 2013 Estimate of Distributor Sales, http://www.ppai.org/inside-ppai/research/Documents/2013%20SalesVolume%20Sheet.pdf.

45 Staff, "State of the Industry," *Counselor Magazine*, ASI, July 1977, page 58.

46 Logos and advertising copy are applied to promotional products in many different ways, including screen printing, hot stamping, engraving, embossing, laser etching, and decal application.

47 This production lead time did not include the time it took to mail the order to the supplier. In that late '70s and early '80s, most suppliers and distributors did not even have fax machines.

48 Lauren A. Murray, *Monthly Labor Review*, Volume 118, August 1995, page 2, http://www.bls.gov/mlr/1995/08/art6full.pdf

49 Named for its sponsor, Ellis Berry, who served as South Dakota's western district congressman from 1951–1971, the Berry Amendment restricts the Department of Defense from using funds to procure certain goods that are not grown, processed, or produced in the United States.

Chapter 3

50 Sun Tzu, The Art of War, translated by Thomas Cleary, Boston, MA, Shambala Publications, 1988, page 41.

51 Eva Dou, "China's New Phone Giant Takes Aim at the World," *Wall Street Journal*, June 8, 2015, page A1.

52 Staff, "A Preview of the MIT Production in the Innovation Economy Report," Production in the Innovation Economy Commission (PIE), Massachusetts Institute of Technology, 2013, page 25.

53 Gary Pisano and Willy Shih, "Producing Prosperity," Harvard Business Review Press, Boston, MA, October 2012, page 102.

54 Staff, "China and the U.S. Economy: Advancing a Winning Trade Agenda," The US-China Business Council, January 2013, page 2.

55 Staff, "Supply Chain Innovation: Strengthening America's Small Manufacturers," Department of Commerce, March 2015, page 13, http://www.esa.doc.gov/sites/default/files/supply_chain_innovation_report.pdf.

56 Daniel Patrick Moynihan.

57 David Nakamura, "Obama hopes to enlist GOP in push for trade pact, despite Democratic resistance," Washington Post, December 26, 2014, https://www.washingtonpost.com/politics/obama-hopes-to-enlist-gop-in-push-for-trade-pact-despite-democratic-resistance/2014/12/26/81236a34-8600-11e4-b9b7-b8632ae73d25_story.html

58 Robert D. Atkinson, Luke A. Stewart, Scott M. Andes, Stephen J. Ezell, "Worse Than the Great Depression: What Experts are Missing About American Manufacturing Decline," The Information Technology & Innovation Foundation, March 2012, page 29, http://www2.itif.org/2012-american-manufacturing-decline.pdf

59 Charles Duhigg, KeithBradsher, "How the U.S. Lost Out on iPhone Work," New York Times, January 21, 2012, http://www.nytimes.com/2012/01/22/business/apple-america-and-a-squeezed-middle-class.html

Chapter 4

60 Sun Tzu, The Art of War, translated by Thomas Cleary, Boston, MA, Shambala Publications, 1988, page 102.

61 Joe Flint, "The Cable Bundle Is Dead. Long Live the Cable Bundle," *Wall Street Journal*, June 9, 2015, page B1.

62 Chris Anderson, *The Long Tail—Why the Future of Business Is Selling Less of More*, Hyperion, New York, NY, 2006, page 52.

63 Kevin O'Marah, "Mass Customization and the Factory of the Future," Industry Week, January 14, 2015, http://www.industryweek.com/factory-of-future.

64 Linda Tischler, "China Knows It Must Innovate But Can It?" Fast Company, September 6, 2011, http://www.fastcodesign.com/1664945/china-knows-it-must-innovate-but-can-it.

65 Beth Macy, *Factory Man*, Little Brown and Company, New York, NY, 2014, page 320.

66 Ibid., pages 339–340.

67 Janice Wang, "Small Runs, Big Gains: Reshoring U.S. Apparel Manufacturing," *Apparel*, January 13, 2015, http://apparel.edgl.com/news/Small-Runs,-Big-Gains---Reshoring-U-S--Apparel-Manufacturing97649.

68 Travis Hessman, "Have It Your Way: Manufacturing in the Age of Mass Customization," *Industry Week*, *Penton*, June 3, 2014.

69 Staff, "Gartner says Worldwide Shipments of 3D Printers to Reach More Than 490,000 in 2016," Gartner Newsroom, September 29, 2015, http://www.gartner.com/newsroom/id/3139118

70 Eddie Krassenstein, "Under Armour's Game Changer is Coming! – 3D Printing Will Usher in a Revolution in Clothing," 3Dprint.com, July 14, 2014, http://3dprint.com/8722/under-armour-3d-printing/

71 Andrew Wheeler, "Half 3D Printed, Half Leather. Oh My God, 3D Printed Shoes," 3D Printing Industry, January 27, 2015, http://3dprintingindustry.com/2015/01/27/half-leather-3d-printed-delcams-3d-printed-shoes/.

72 Juliana Goldman, "Taking a Test Drive in a 3D Printed Car," CBS News, January 24, 2015, http://www.cbsnews.com/videos/taking-a-test-drive-in-a-3d-printed-car/.

73 RH Editors, "3D Food Edges Closer to Reality for Restaurants," *Restaurant Hospitality*, January 16, 2015, http://restaurant-hospitality.com/food-trends/3d-food-edges-closer-reality-restaurants?NL=NED-19&Issue=NED-19_20150105_NED-9_304_CPY1&sfvc4enews=42&cl=article_3_3&YM_RID=CPG03000001472225&YM_MID=2984.

74 Margot Peppers, "Custom cookies at the click of a button: Oreo vending machine uses 3D printing technology to create personalized treats," DailyMail.com, March 12, 2014, http://www.dailymail.co.uk/femail/article-2578658/Custom-cookies-click-button-Oreo-vending-machine-uses-3D-printing-technology-create-personalized-treats.html

75 Staff, "Clothing Printer Concept for 2050 Allows You to Produce Your Own Clothes from Home," Tuvie Design of the Future, http://www.tuvie.com/clothing-printer-concept-for-2050-allows-you-to-produce-your-own-clothes-from-home/.

76 Joseph Flaherty, "This Dress Is Made from 3D Printed Plastic, But Flows Like Fabric," Wired, December 9, 2014, http://www.wired.com/2014/12/dress-made-3-d-printed-plastic-flows-like-fabric/.

77 Chris Anderson, *The Long Tail—Why the Future of Business Is Selling Less of More*, Hyperion, New York, NY, 2006, page 82.

Chapter 5

78 Sun Tzu, *The Art of War*, translated by Thomas Cleary, Boston, MA, Shambala Publications, 1988, page 53.

79 Lee Matthews, "U.S. Postal Service Selects Drone as Potential New Delivery Vehicle," Geek.com, April 21, 2015, http://www.geek.com/news/u-s-postal-service-selects-drone-as-potential-new-delivery-vehicle-1620904/.

80 Ron Johnson, "Reshoring Brings Jobs Back to U.S., including Pensacola," *Pensacola News Journal*, January 17, 2015, http://www.pnj.com/story/news/2015/01/17/reshoring-brings-jobs-back-us-including-pensacola/21929659/

81 Lorraine Mirabella, "Under Armour's vision for future manufacturing: make local for local," *Baltimore Sun*, October 10, 2015, http://www.baltimoresun.com/business/bs-bz-under-armour-local-manufacturing-20151010-story.html

82 Michael Connerty and Carol Wingard, "American Manufacturing: Not a New Dawn But a Welcome Advance," *Industry Week*, December 17, 2014, http://www.industryweek.com/competitiveness/american-manufacturing-not-new-dawn-welcome-advance

83. Marc Bain, "The Neurological Pleasures of Fast Fashion," *Atlantic*, March 25, 2015, http://www.theatlantic.com/entertainment/archive/2015/03/the-neurological-pleasures-of-modern-shopping/388577/.
84. Clare O'Connor, "These Retailers Involved In Bangladesh Factory Disaster Have Yet To Compensate Victims," *Forbes*, April 26, 2014, http://www.forbes.com/sites/clareoconnor/2014/04/26/these-retailers-involved-in-bangladesh-factory-disaster-have-yet-to-compensate-victims/
85. Staff, "21 million people are now victims of forced labour, ILO says," ILO Press Release, June 1, 2012, http://www.ilo.org/global/about-the-ilo/newsroom/news/WCMS_181961/lang--en/index.htm

Chapter 6

86. Sun Tzu, The Art of War, translated by Thomas Cleary, Boston, MA, Shambala Publications, 1988, page 52.
87. Interviews with Raelynn Hughes, September 2012.
88. Ibid, September 2012.
89. Eric B. Lipton and David Barboza, "As More Toys Are Recalled, Trail Ends in China," *New York Times*, June 19, 2007, http://www.nytimes.com/2007/06/19/business/worldbusiness/19toys.html?pagewanted=all&_r=0.
90. Nick Leiber and David Rocks, "Small U.S. Manufacturers Give Up on 'Made in China,'" *Bloomberg Businessweek*, June 26, 2012, http://www.bloomberg.com/news/articles/2012-06-22/small-u-s-manufacturers-give-up-on-made-in-china-.
91. Paul Mooney, "The Story Behind China's Tainted Milk Scandal," *U.S. News*, October 9, 2008, http://www.usnews.com/news/world/articles/2008/10/09/the-story-behind-chinas-tainted-milk-scandal.
92. Edward Wong, "China: Inquiry on Tainted Milk Powder," *New York Times*, January 14, 2011, http://www.nytimes.com/2011/01/15/world/asia/15briefs-Milk.html.
93. Mark McDonald, "Carcinogen Found in Chinese Baby Formula," *New York Times*, July 23, 2012, http://rendezvous.blogs.nytimes.com/2012/07/23/carcinogen-found-in-chinese-baby-formula/.
94. Shaun Rein, *The End of Cheap China*, John Wiley & Sons, Inc., Hoboken, NJ, 2012, page 98.
95. Hughes interviews, September 2012.

Chapter 7

96. Cynthia Drummond, "Hopkinton council forgives taxes, questions RhodeMap vote," *The Westerly Sun*, December 16, 2014, http://www.thewesterlysun.com/news/latestnews/6438102-129/hopkinton-council-forgives-taxes-questions-rhodemap-vote.html

97 Sun Tzu, The Art of War, translated by Thomas Cleary, Boston, MA, Shambala Publications, 1988, page 43.
98 Staff, "Raleigh Denim Featured in October Whole Living Magazine," eco-chick.com, October 4, 2012, http://eco-chick.com/2012/10/11999/raleigh-denim-featured-in-october-whole-living-magazine/
99 Interview with Dana Floyd, September 2015.
100 Alana Semuels, "'Good Jobs' Aren't Coming Back," *Atlantic*, October 26, 2015, http://www.theatlantic.com/business/archive/2015/10/onshoring-jobs/412201/.

Chapter 8

101 Sun Tzu, The Art of War, translated by Thomas Cleary, Boston, MA, Shambala Publications, 1988, page 125.
102 Associated Press, "Lincolnton Furniture Company Closes One Year after Being Hailed by Obama as U.S. Job Creator," *Huffington Post*, January 4, 2013, http://www.huffingtonpost.com/2013/01/04/lincolnton-furniture-company-closes_n_2410463.html.
103 Staff, "Supply Chain Innovation: Strengthening Americas Small Manufacturers," U.S. Commerce Department, March 2015, page 13, https://www.whitehouse.gov/sites/default/files/docs/supply_chain_innovation_report_final.pdf
104 http://www.d2pbuyersguide.com/
105 "Small Empires: Makers Row and the Future of American Manufacturing," Posted October 29, 2013, https://www.youtube.com/watch?v=ADYL-7lNlcs.
106 U.S. Department of Labor, Bureau of Internal Affairs, List of Goods Produced by Child Labor or Forced Labor, http://www.dol.gov/ilab/reports/child-labor/list-of-goods/.
107 Lisa Fickenscher, "Just in Time for July 4th, Walmart Caught in an Un-American Lie," *New York Post*, June 29, 2015, http://nypost.com/2015/06/29/walmart-sold-us-made-products-that-were-actually-foreign/.

Chapter 9

108 Sun Tzu, The Art of War, translated by Thomas Cleary, Boston, MA, Shambala Publications, 1988, page 78.
109 Madeleine Morgenstern, "Oops: Keychains Touting Missouri Jobs Initiative Actually 'Made in China,'" The Blaze, August 12, 2011, http://www.theblaze.com/stories/2011/08/12/oops-keychains-touting-missouri-jobs-initiative-actually-made-in-china/
110 https://research.stlouisfed.org/fred2/series/MEHOINUSA672N
111 Staff, "Food Imports to United States Soar under WTO-NAFTA Model, Threatening American Farmers and Safety," Public Citizen, June 2014, http://www.citizen.org/documents/food-under-nafta-wto.pdf.

112 Alan Farnham, "Seafood from Asia Raised on Pig Waste, Says News Report," ABC World News, October 17, 2012, http://abcnews.go.com/Business/consumers-eating-feces-tainted-shrimp-fish-seafood-asia/story?id=17491264.

113 Staff, "Food Imports to United States Soar under WTO-NAFTA Model, Threatening American Farmers and Safety," Public Citizen, June 2014, http://www.citizen.org/documents/food-under-nafta-wto.pdf

114 David Kesmodel, William Mauldin, Jonathan D. Rockoff, "Historic Trade Deal Sealed," *Wall Street Journal*, October 6, 2015, page A2.

115 C. Fred Bergsten and Maurice Greenberg, "The U.S. Needs a Free-Trade Deal with China," *Wall Street Journal*, December 18, 2014, http://www.wsj.com/articles/maurice-greenberg-and-fred-bergsten-the-u-s-needs-a-free-trade-deal-with-china-1418946345.

116 U.S.-China Economic and Security Review Commission, 2014 Report to Congress, Executive Summary, page 4.

117 Ibid., page 12.

118 Staff, "2015 Report to Congress of the U.S.-China Economic and Security Review Commission, Executive Summary and Recommendations" U.S.-China Economic and Security Review Commission, November 2015, page viii, http://origin.www.uscc.gov/sites/default/files/annual_reports/2015%20Executive%20Summary%20and%20Recommendations.pdf

119 Ibid., page 20.

120 Ibid., page 9.

121 Richard D'Aveni, *Strategic Capitalism—The New Economic Strategy for Winning the Capitalist Cold War*, McGraw-Hill, New York, NY, 2012, page 53.

122 Paul Mozur, "New Rules in China Upset Western Tech Companies," *New York Times*, January 28, 2015, http://www.nytimes.com/2015/01/29/technology/in-china-new-cybersecurity-rules-perturb-western-tech-companies.html?_r=0

123 Ivan Kenneally, "Chinese Central Bank Depreciates Yuan; Plans to Rival the U.S. Dollar," *Sourcing Journal Online*, March 3, 2014, https://www.sourcingjournalonline.com/chinese-central-banks-depreciates-yuan-plans-rival-u-s-dollar/.

124 Staff, "New Senate Finance Chairman Sets Markers on Trade Policy," Sandler, Travis & Rosenberg Trade Report, April 11, 2014, http://www.strtrade.com/news-publications-Wyden-trade-policy-TPA-FTA-041114.html

125 Kathleen Miller, "Sept. 11 Bracelets Come From China Amid 'Buy America' Loopholes," Bloomberg Business, January 10, 2012, http://www.bloomberg.com/news/articles/2012-01-10/sept-11-bracelets-come-from-china

126 Staff, "New 'Buy American' Rules May Be on the Horizon," *Law 360*, September 24, 2014, http://www.law360.com/articles/579348/new-buy-american-rules-may-be-on-the-horizon.

127 Ana Radelat, "Murphy has win in 'Buy America' campaign," The CT Mirror, June 18, 2015, http://ctmirror.org/2015/06/18/murphy-has-win-in-buy-american-campaign/
128 John Stossel, "The Stupidity of 'Buy American,'" Reason.com, November 3, 2011, https://reason.com/archives/2011/11/03/the-stupidity-of-buy-american
129 The Narrow Fabrics Institute (NFI) is predominantly comprised of US-based manufacturers of narrow web products. NFI is a division of the Industrial Fabrics Association International (IFAI). http://narrowfabrics.ifai.com/
130 Nguyen Dieu Tu Uyen, "Asian Seafood Raised on Pig Feces Approved for U.S. Consumers," *Bloomberg Business*, October 11, 2012, http://www.bloomberg.com/news/articles/2012-10-11/asian-seafood-raised-on-pig-feces-approved-for-u-s-consumers.
131 Nish Amarnath, "Curt Schilling's 38 Studios: Rhode Island On The Hook For $112 Million, Chafee Calls For Audit," *International Business Times*, June 27, 2012, http://www.ibtimes.com/curt-schillings-38-studios-rhode-island-hook-112-million-chafee-calls-audit-704631
132 Joe Stephens and Carol D. Leonnig, "Solyndra: Politics Infused Obama Energy Programs," *Washington Post*, December 25, 2011, http://www.washingtonpost.com/solyndra-politics-infused-obama-energy-programs/2011/12/14/gIQA4HllHP_story.html.
133 Staff, "2013 Report Card for America's Infrastructure," American Society of Civil Engineers, http://www.infrastructurereportcard.org/
134 Bob Patterson and James Pinkerton, "A Vision of American Strength: How Infrastructure Built the United States," page 94.
135 Garry Kasparov and Peter Thiel, "Our Dangerous Illusion of Tech Progress," *Financial Times*, November 8, 2012, http://www.ft.com/cms/s/0/8adeca00-2996-11e2-a5ca-00144feabdc0.html#axzz3g4WD03Ql.
136 Richard D'Aveni, Strategic Capitalism—The New Economic Strategy for Winning the Capitalist Cold War, McGraw-Hill, New York, NY, 2012, page 154.